CONRAD TO A FRIEND

CONRAD
TO A FRIEND

150 SELECTED LETTERS FROM JOSEPH
CONRAD TO RICHARD CURLE

EDITED WITH AN INTRODUCTION AND
NOTES BY R. C.

"I suspect that you keep
my letters and may some
day deliver them to the
printer's devil."

J. C. *to* **R. C.**
August 20th, 1916

NEW YORK / RUSSELL & RUSSELL

To

R. B. CUNNINGHAME GRAHAM

the recipient of many of Conrad's

most delightful letters

PREFACE TO THE 1968 PRINTING

LETTERS speak for themselves, and anyone reading these letters will, I feel sure, perceive that the general impression they convey is of a friendship which, throughout the years, grew into close confidence and understanding. I wrote in my original introduction to this collection of letters, "As I read them again they recover for me a hundred moods and incidents, they recall to me his speaking voice, they give me back the very aspect of his physical presence." But there was more to it than that: they keenly awaken again the sense of a loss I mourn to this day.

I fear I was rather a trying correspondent at times, particularly in my efforts to write effectively about his work, but even when he had to correct me, which, quite rightly, was often, he was always friendly in his judicious advice. And yet, though there is much literary criticism in it, this is not basically a literary correspondence. No, it is, in its essence, a record of companionship, enlivened by Conrad's masterly touch. And therein lies such value as it possesses, for it exhibits Conrad as a human being, not a towering figure, and reveals for all to see his kindliness, his consideration for others, his gift of friendship. Despite a high-strung nervous temperament, occasionally flaring into sharp annoyance or ironic contempt, his usual manner was humorously easy and mildly interested in the world around him.

But in the mind of so teeming and profound a creative artist, with its hidden depths of incommunicable aloofness, may it not be that external trivialities acted as a sort of anodyne? Sometimes of an evening, when he and I were sitting in his study after dinner, I seemed to glimpse another Conrad altogether. His talk would trail off into reminiscence, his voice, attuned to his mood, would assume a dreamy tone, and a panorama of the past, conjured, as it were, out of his subconscious musings, would unfold itself from the abyss of memory.

I am not, of course, claiming for a moment that such incidents disclosed even the ghost of the innermost Conrad, but only that what he was describing was so obviously bound up with the very fibre of his work that it was clearly an echo of something deep within himself. But the revelations would cease as mysteriously as they had begun, and all at once he would be back in the present, as if one figure had melted into another.

Those evenings are precious to recall, but so, indeed, is all the time I spent with Conrad. For he was the ideal friend and the ideal host. There was a total absence of pose about him and he never mentioned his books in company unless asked questions, while with his pervasive charm he made every visitor feel at home. And this was not merely on the surface: such men as John Galsworthy, R. B. Cunninghame Graham, Hugh Clifford, Edward Garnett and Sydney Colvin had been his close friends for many years.

Even in a simple correspondence such as this, one feels the power of Conrad's personality, and in his actual presence its unique, compelling quality stimulated all who met him. In a room crowded with people he stood forth effortlessly, and though his conversation was brilliant and ranging, yet it was not, I fancy, the richness of his talk which so signalled him out, but something in himself that entirely defied definition. Oustanding personality is an inherent endowment, and had Conrad never written a line he would still have been regarded as a very remarkable man. And when, added to this, he was so sympathetic and helpful, so full of concern for those he cared about, how could I not have cherished his friendship. It is one of my proudest memories.

That is the kind of man he was, and it is to show him in this light, and suggest, if my words are at all adequate, the vividness of his personality, that these letters, with my two Introductions, seem to me to be well worth reprinting.

January, 1968   RICHARD CURLE

INTRODUCTION

THE 150 letters contained in this volume have been selected from the large number that Conrad wrote to me from the year in which I first met him, 1912, to the year of his death, 1924. Only ten* of these letters have been printed in the official *Life and Letters,* and those ten were, I think, chosen by the editor more for the facts they contain than for their quality as letters. Therefore the correspondence is, practically speaking, unknown; and I think that, if for no other reason, it is worth preserving in this form as presenting an angle of Conrad that few of his letters so far published do present.

It is not a literary correspondence in essentials, nor is it the type of correspondence one conducts with a friend whom one seldom sees. Indeed, I would have received many more letters from Conrad but for the fact that for some years of the period in which I knew him I was far from England and that he wrote to me only sparingly during such absences. His correspondence with me was of so familiar a kind that distance put a natural curb upon it: you cannot, as it were, talk easily to a man across several thousand miles. Or to a wanderer—I find, from his envelopes that he wrote to me to eighteen different addresses.

When I was really settled in England, on the other hand,

---

*Those dated Nov. 6, 1912, Nov. 6, 1913, April 1914, July 4, 1914, Aug. 20, 1916, Oct. 1922, May 11, 1923, July 14, 1923, July 17, 1923, and Aug. 22, 1923.

Conrad was constantly sending me short notes about his doings and his thoughts, and those notes have the value of showing us his life as it passed from day to day. They give innumerable glimpses of his activities and his opinions, and they are attractive, taken all in all, rather as a revelation of an unclouded friendship than as a display of Conrad's genius for letter writing.

I am talking about the correspondence as a whole, because now and again, when specially aroused, Conrad would send me very long letters; and that would also happen when I was abroad. But I have not hesitated to put side by side with such letters notes of the briefest description, similar to the words friends throw at one another across a table. Of course, I have not printed all such notes, for there would be no purpose in endless repetition, but I do think that a sprinkling of them conveys satisfactorily the intimate tone of the correspondence. And it is not alone trivial notes that I have omitted: some of Conrad's letters to me are irretrievably lost, others are entirely taken up with his or my private affairs. And I have not included every letter he wrote me about my long illness: there is only too much to do with illness in Conrad's own family in these letters.

Nearly all Conrad's letters to me were written in his own hand; not more than about a dozen were dictated. He liked to give them the extra touch of personality that comes from handwriting. And for that reason I have, while punctuating the letters to some extent, left Conrad's abbreviations as he wrote them. It seems to me that they heighten the flavour of the letters and make Conrad live more vividly within the sentences. He had in truth developed a regular system of shortening words, which, on occasion, could be both bewildering and individual.

These letters, read as a unit, are like a running commentary on the last dozen years of Conrad's life. They reflect his particular kind of humour, his affectionate nature, and his constant concern for his friends. They reveal him in a very human light, and they prove that he was a man who had a clear grasp of affairs. They round off the picture of Conrad in a manner which more impersonal and more persistently brilliant letters could not do.

At his best Conrad was a great letter writer, as I imagine all readers of his *Life and Letters* will admit. His ironic mind plays over his correspondence, and in those letters flung off at odd moments there is a mastery of expression that is astonishing. In them one hears the authentic Conrad, in whom the grand manner and a personal charm were mixed with such singular felicity.

I have been at particular pains to see that the text is accurate: nothing could be more pointless than incorrectly printed letters. But that does not mean that they are, in all cases, given in full or even nearly in full. It stands to reason that in an unfettered correspondence such as his, in which Conrad spoke freely of other people and of his own affairs, there were many remarks which it would be indiscreet to publish, and many which would be of small interest to the general reader. A properly edited correspondence is inevitably selective.

What with gout in his wrist and the demands on his time, letter writing was a real labour to Conrad. All the same, it was a labour that he never shirked. There can have been few men who put so much of themselves into their letters and so regularly kept in touch with their friends through the medium of the written word.

Conrad had a large number of friends and a host of unknown admirers, and he wrote many letters. Indeed, he was not at all the indifferent recluse that people have supposed, but was extremely punctilious in the matter of replying to inquiries and answering sensible questions. Several thousands of his letters are known to be in existence, and gradually, no doubt, more and more of these will be printed. And that is all to the good, for they have a finish and a wisdom of their own. I should not be surprised if in future years his correspondence became an integral part of his published works.

But, as I said before, I do not print these letters mainly for their literary quality—some of his letters to strangers are, in the nature of things, more literary than most of these—but as a remembrance of a most precious friendship. As I read them again they recover for me a hundred moods and incidents, they recall to me his speaking voice, they give me back the very aspect of his physical presence. Just as in conversation no one could buttonhole a friend more perfectly than Conrad, so even in his slightest note one felt the close reality of his friendship. It is my hope that these letters may succeed in showing Conrad to others with some of the vividness that they show him again to me.

RICHARD CURLE.

LETTERS

12 March '23

Dearest Dick. Pardon this
scrap of paper. It is but
to send you my congratulations on reaching the mature
age of 40 — and to thank
you for the copy of the special edition received today.
I like the appearance very
much. I hope the book will
meet with the recognition it deserves.

I have begun today an
introduction to a forthcoming
biography of Crane by a man
called Beer. He and Knopf came
here on Thursday last on that
business — which is in truth
a marvellously good business
for me. I want to give him
about 3500 words. It

Will take some doing, tho'.

I am sorry to see from Jessie's letter that you cannot come over with me into the Land of the Mohicans. I have a short note from F.N.D. (from the Bahamas). The letter in which I announced your possible arrival with me had not reached him yet when he wrote. He must have it now. He intends to be back long before the date of the voyage of the New Columbus (without Pinzon!! ?)

Can't get up any enthusiasm for it. More details, when we meet — which will have to be soon.

Ever Yrs J. Conrad.

Capel House,
Orlestone,
nr. Ashford.
6. Nov. '12.

My dear Mr. Curle,

I need have been an ungrateful churl not to
be moved by your article for the *Rhythm*.[1] A mere sympathetic attempt would have been something to be thank-
ful for—but you have very definitely achieved an analysis which (whatever others may think of it) I hold as
very valuable both in matter and tone. A great friend of
mine [2] said to me the other day: "This is the first thing
worth reading which has been written about you in the
way of general appreciation."

Garnett [3] tells me that you would find time to
run down here for a day and night. We'll be very glad to
see you here if you don't mind the grind of the journey.
I shall drop you a line before very long suggesting a day.
I am not very well now and don't come downstairs, though
not actually laid up. Meantime I thank you heartily for

---

(1) The article he refers to appeared in *Rhythm*, November, 1912.
What pleased Conrad especially was that this article was mainly
about *Nostromo*, the novel which he himself called his "largest can-
vas," but which had been much neglected by the critics.

(2) I fancy this "great friend" may have been his neighbour,
Arthur Marwood, of whose critical powers he had the highest
opinion.

(3) Edward Garnett, who had been Fisher Unwin's reader when
Almayer's Folly was submitted to him. It was on his advice that it
was published.

your more than in one way very interesting vol.[4] We shall have a talk about it when you come with the corpus delicti there before us, to refer to.

Glad you like old Jacobus [5]—the impure Jacobus.

Kind regards,

Yours sincerely,

J. CONRAD.

(4) The volume he refers to is my book of short stories, *Shadows out of the Crowd.*

(5) One of the principal characters in "A Smile of Fortune." This was the first letter I received from Conrad.

Capel House,
Orlestone,
nr. Ashford.
Saturday, [23rd November, 1912.]

My dear Mr. Curle,

Many thanks for your letter and the paper.[1]
The p.-card turned up this afternoon. I assure you I appreciate everything you have written of my work immensely.

Would the 6th Dec. suit you for running down here? Suppose you take the 4.20 from Char. X., arrives here 6.9. We would have a long talk into the night and you could return by the 9.54 next morning. In fixing the hours like this I treat you as an old friend.[2] I had six blank weeks and am hopelessly behind with my work. If the date doesn't suit please mention another—earlier or later.

Pardon this hurried scrawl.

Yours cordially,
J. CONRAD.

---

(1) *Everyman* for November 22nd, 1912, containing an article by me entitled "The Art of Joseph Conrad."

(2) A figure of speech of course, but I think I had actually met Conrad for a second time between the date of this letter and the previous one. I met him first at the Mont Blanc restaurant, Gerrard Street, London, at the invitation of Edward Garnett. When Conrad was in town he used occasionally to go to lunch at this restaurant for the purpose of meeting Edward Garnett, W. H. Hudson, and other literary men, who used to assemble there one day a week.

Capel House,
Orlestone,
nr. Ashford.
Wednesday, [December, 1912.]

Excellentissimo Señor,

Since you will not come [1] without this additional guarantee of good faith, the present is to inform that we are expecting you on Friday next by the train arriving in Hamstreet (change in Ashford—next station) at 6.9.

If you don't see me at the Station you'll find there a puffer of archaic aspect and wheezy constitution.

Au revoir then.

Yours,
J. C.

---

(1) This refers, I fancy, to my as yet unmade first visit to Conrad.

[Capel House.]
Friday, [31st March, 1913.]

My dear Curle,

Pardon the delay. In the matter of article about *Nostromo* [1] Pinker,[2] thinks that if you do write it he could place it with the *North Am. Review*. This would be more satisfactory than entrusting *Harper's* with it. The last will be always a second string.

No. I have no articles on my work. I don't keep these things.

I am feeling very flat. My manner is evolving into something new to which I am not used. The work in such conditions comes with difficulty and the doubt as to his [its] value is worrying.

Our kindest regards,

Yours,

J. CONRAD.

---

(1) After all I did not write the article at the time. I finally wrote it as an introduction to the volume containing *Nostromo* in the Memorial Edition, published in 1925.

(2) J. B. Pinker, Conrad's Literary Agent.

[Capel House.]
Friday, [13th July, 1913.]

My dear Curle,

Pink[1] must have thought I was staying with you. Will you drop him a line to say if the day and hour suit you.

I've been desperately busy with proofs[2] since my return here.

Pardon this scrap of paper.

Yours in haste.

J. CONRAD.

(1) Conrad's familiar name for the late J. B. Pinker.
(2) The proofs of *Chance*.

[Capel House.]
Friday, [July, 1913.]

My dear Curle,

I am glad you've hit it off with Pink.

Very good of you to have written to me. My dear fellow, I am unaffectedly glad to know that you are undertaking the task.[1] All I can say is that when you want me for anything I am at your disposal—to give information or elucidate a point. I say this without reserve because I feel a complete confidence in you.

On my part I have written Doubleday (in America), my future publisher there, saying that you are about to write such a book and that I would wish them to publish it. More I couldn't say just at present.

If, for instance, the Yank press receives your study of Conrad well there would be an opening for you then to write about other Europeans of letters—the sort of nourishment they need much, and of which, one must render them justice, they are rather greedy.

Once your name becomes familiar to their democratic ear, they will be ready for reception of stories and novels. Great thing is to affirm your existence first.

I've just passed two sets of proofs of *Chance*. My brain's muddled, my spirits depressed. I had to read that stuff so many times over that I have lost all belief in it.

(1) Refers to the study of Conrad which I was anxious to write. It was finally published in 1914 by Doubleday, Page in America and by Kegan Paul in England.

My other work has been neglected meantime, I feel wretched.

It's late. No more. Good luck to you.

Yours affectionately,

J. CONRAD.

Tuesday. ev.
Capel House,
Orlestone,
nr. Ashford.
[15th July, 1913.]

My dear Curle,

May I come to see you—in fact, for lunch—to-morrow, *Wednesday*. This time I will be alone. I beg and pray that if it is in the slightest way inconvenient you will drop me a wire care *Bookishly London*[1] about ten o'clock. I would, *if allowed*, come early, soon after 12 o'clock and stay till 3; when I may have to see a man (but not about a dog). Having to come up for business, I start earlier on purpose to see you if possible.

Affectionately yours,
J. CONRAD.

---

(1) Pinker's telegraphic address.

Capel House,
Orlestone,
nr. Ashford.
26 Augt. '13.

My dear Curle,

Just a word to thank you for your letter. I
am glad to hear your party is having a good time.[1]

It is very good of you to tell me so much of
your work on me.[2] Certainly, my dear fellow, you must
come here when you like and as often as you think a talk
may be of some help to you. That you will do something
of value and significance in the way of criticism I have no
doubt. I consider myself fortunate in your appreciation
of my work. What you say of the blank Mandarinism of
our contemporary critics is very true. Perhaps your book
on my writings may be the means of making a hole in the
Chinese Wall and letting in some fresh air into that stuffy
region.

Chance will appear some twenty days hence[3]—in time
for you to read it in book form. I shall order an early
copy to be sent to you at your town address. As to your
wish to see the MS. of the "D" novel[4] (the one I am
writing now), I can have no hesitation to let you see it—

---

(1) I was then in the Channel Islands on holiday.

(2) This refers to my proposed book on Conrad, for which I was
then studying.

(3) It was first published in England in the middle of September, 1913, but that edition was withdrawn, and it was not finally
published till February, 1914.

(4) Evidently *Victory.*

of course. But I question the necessity. We must talk it over when we meet. In the matter of my uncollected stuff (it's a very small amount) I should say: decidedly not. It isn't worth while taking it into account.[5] It would bring a needless complication into your general view of J. C. and your particular analysis of his prose. These things are without importance. I don't think it would be even *good policy* to bring them into your survey.

      With affection,

              Yours,

                J. CONRAD.

P.S. You cannot doubt that it would please me immensely to have *Chance* reviewed in the press by you.[6] But won't it put you off your work? Don't do anything to interfere with the continuity of your mood.

---

(5) I had suggested that I should make a study of Conrad's uncollected articles for the purpose of my book.

(6) I reviewed *Chance* in two papers, the *English Review* and the *Bookman*, both in February, 1914.

[Capel House,] 6 Nov. 13.

My dear Curle,

Many thanks for the chapter on Women.[1] Frankly it pleases it [me] much and it also pleases my wife—so you have achieved a feat which is commonly regarded as impossible.

There is nothing there that I could take exception to even in the innermost of my feelings. Of course not. Your evident sympathy cheers me immensely and your acuteness comes out wonderfully in the simplicity of your style. The "voice" is perfect to my mind. About what it says you know my feeling. But in one respect, my dear Curle, I beg you most earnestly to follow my advice; and it is this: that all the notes should be incorporated into the text.[2] They will fall into their places admirably, without any trouble. They belong there. It's judgment or comment—part of your developed appreciation. Then why exile them and distract the eye of the reader—and by breaking the flow of the page impoverish the effect of the text? I won't say anything on the appearance of formality it introduces into what is meant to be, and indeed is, an intimate study meant for the general public.

I keep the chap. for a day or so more. And I shall send it back to Chelsea.

Affectionate regards from us both,

Yours in haste,

J. CONRAD.

(1) One of the chapters in my book on Conrad.

(2) I followed his advice.

[Capel House.]
7 Jan. '14.

My dear Curle,

I have read and have been touched deeply in places by the sympathetic understanding of my work you display all along.[1] I have 3 remarks to make in all, of which two [are] of minor order. The third will be for your conscience to accept or reject.

You must, of course, come here. Will you pardon me if I don't suggest a day immediately? I am finishing a short story of some importance[2] and I hope to be done on Monday. I'll write you at once then, giving you a choice of days. But you'll have to come to sleep, as the evening will be the best time for our talk.

Wife sends kind regards.

Yours ever,
J. CONRAD.

---

(1) This evidently refers to the complete MS. of my book on his work.

(2) One of the stories of *Within the Tides.*

[Capel House.]
[February, 1914.]

My dear Curle,

Thanks. I made one correction in the bibliography.[1]

I have been ailing with gout for upwards of a month. No work done and no end of worry.

Our love to you.

Yours ever,
J. CONRAD.

(1) The skeleton bibliography at the end of my book on Conrad.

Capel House,
Orlestone,
nr. Ashford.
Tuesday, [February, 1914.]

Dear Curle,

Pardon the delay.

I've made a few corrections (printer's) and one on p. 17 which is *important* for the sense.[1]

Many thanks.

Yours affectionately,
J. CONRAD.

---

(1) This refers to the proofs of my book on Conrad, which I had sent him.

[Capel House.]
Monday, [30th March, 1914.]

My dear Curle,

I answer at once that the idea pleases me.[1]
Just give it another spell of consideration and then if it
still commends itself to you, well—go ahead.

But please reflect that it might give occasion
for nasty people saying I helped to get up the book. As
a matter of fact, I don't care personally. Think of your
own position please.

Our kindest regards,

Affectionately yours,

J. Conrad.

I keep the two books a little longer. Shakes^re very
good.[2]

---

(1) I had asked Conrad's permission to reprint the Suppressed
Preface to *The Nigger of the "Narcissus,"* which was not at that
time obtainable.

(2) I had lent Conrad Bradley's book, *Shakespearean Tragedy.*

[Capel House.]
31st Mch, [1914.]

My dear Curle,

I've been thinking the blessed thing out—
and, do you know, I really believe it would be better to
leave the preface alone. It isn't dans la note of your book
—it would sound declamatory, even windy, against your
pages.[1]

I don't like to negative anything you like to
do—but still!

Anyway, if you do, ask first Heinemann's permission, as the late owners of the *New Review*, and then
state (in a note) that you have extracted it from there
(*N. Review*).

Affectionately yours,
J. CONRAD.

---

(1) Conrad, as can be seen, had now changed his mind as to the
desirability of reprinting the Suppressed Preface. It was in the *New
Review* that it appeared when *The Nigger of the "Narcissus"* was
serialised there in 1897.

[Capel House.]
Monday, [April, 1914.]

My dear Curle,

Herewith the corrected page. Sorry I kept it over Sunday.

The *Times'* review is indeed intelligent (if incomplete) in its appreciation.[1]

My blessing on your labours.

Yours,
J. CONRAD.

(1) A review of my book on Conrad.

[Capel House.]
Thursday, [April, 1914.]

My dear Richard,

I snatch this piece of MS. paper after reception of 2 more reviews to share my impression with you.[1] Well, I must say that the book is receiving a magnificent acknowledgment of its existence anyhow. That you are attacked causes me great pain—but there can be in it for you no sense of defeat. I've told you that you would have brickbats thrown at you. You jostle too many people's idols for my sake. But really with the exception of the . . . (a mere impertinence of no authority) the others, I am delighted to see, all recognise your sincerity, your insight, and every other merit of the book. After the flouts and jeers, which you can't deny you have to a certain extent provoked, there comes always a note of genuine respect for the singleness of purpose, the transparent rectitude of your "pioneer" (as the *Times* points it out) achievement. Of course the small dogs yap the most. They would have yapped at an angel from heaven likewise— and I don't suppose you are much disturbed by that noise. After all, that too is recognition.

As time goes on a reaction is sure to set in, for no amount of envenomed comment can obscure the merit of the work. And the venom too is of very bad quality. It is also the sort of thing that must be discounted because, don't you see, a book of that sort is bound to provoke

---

(1) Conrad is referring to the reviews of my book on him, many of which were very bad. He was trying to cheer me up.

that particular kind of attack from every twopenny mind. If I were sure of how you take it my satisfaction would be complete. Drop me a line soon. I am terrifically busy.

Yours ever,

J. CONRAD.

[Capel House.]
[4th June, 1914.]

My dear Curle,

It was indeed delightful to me to have your excellent, soothing, friendly company through what would have been a very trying day otherwise.

But I wonder what those fellows at *Ill. Lond. News* Office[1] thought you were? From the severity of your demeanour when in that hole of a place they may have thought that Conrad wanted looking after lest he should get drunk and disgrace himself if allowed to wander about town alone. I noticed they looked at you with a sort of awe, and, as it were, concealed curiosity. They were evidently "très intrigués." Awfully funny. Thanks no end for everything you have done and are doing for me, my dearest fellow.

Love from all here.

Yours ever
J. CONRAD.

---

(1) This letter refers to a visit Conrad paid to the office of the *Illustrated London News*, accompanied by myself, in order to read the proofs of his article "The Lesson of the Collision" which appeared in that paper on June 6th, 1914.

Capel House,
Orlestone,
nr. Ashford.
Sunday, [June, 1914.]

My dear Curle,

Will you render me the great service to take my letter[1] to Printing House Sq. and ascertain whether the *Times* will publish it. I don't know if they've pub^d the Nowell[2] letter, but in any case you know how anxious I am for the *Times* to take the matter up.

I've just heard of another collision (apparently on Sat.) between the "New-York" and "Pretoria." If that "P" is still the old ship of that name then she has a beak-bow. The damage is all *above water*, they say. An added argument for the fender. For imagine instead of the hard beak an elastic fender! The damage would have been insignificant.

Yours ever,
J. CONRAD.

Please drop me a line.

---

(1) A letter on the same subject as the article mentioned in the note to the previous letter. Both the article and the letter were written by Conrad as a result of the sinking of the "Empress of Ireland" in a collision at the mouth of the St. Lawrence River. For some reason or other the letter was not printed in the *Times,* but was printed in the *Daily Express*—I presume it is the same letter—June 10, 1914.

(2) Apparently a man who had sent Conrad a letter on this subject. At this time Conrad received numerous letters either controverting or supporting his views.

[Capel House.]
Monday, [July, 1914.]

My dear Richard,

Thanks. I am absolutely plunged, submerged and totally absorbed in the end of the novel.[1]

Whatever happens we will be in Sh^d [Sheffield][2] on the day and hour. You are a real friend!

Yours ever,

J. Conrad.

---

(1) *Victory.*

(2) Conrad's eldest son, Borys, was in for an examination at Sheffield University. I met them both there in order to keep Conrad company.

Capel House,
Orlestone,
nr. Ashford.
22 July '14.

Cher Seigneur,

You have no idea what a terrible task I had in revising and putting into shape the enormous mass of typewritten pages which went to make up that *Victory*.[1] I have been at it up to the 19th, almost without intermission. It was a damnable business. But it's over at last and the monstrous pile is gone to America.

I really had no time to drop you a line. Don't you be angry with me. I understand that Jessie[2] in her gratitude has written to you. As to myself, I am just recovering from the ordeal and want all the sympathy I can get in the period of convalescence.

Everything being finished (and my reason still seated on its throne) I went and had a final interview with Pinker, before our departure.[3] He thinks your book[4] a very excellent piece of work and confessed that reading it has given him pleasure. He isn't a reading man, you know. He is also convinced that the book has not done

(1) *Victory* was published in America in March, 1915, but not published in England till September of that year.

(2) Conrad's wife.

(3) This was his departure, with his wife and two sons, for a visit to Poland—the first for many years. The War caught him in Poland, and he found great difficulty in returning to England *via* Italy.

(4) My book on Conrad.

you harm—on the contrary. It has been much talked about and he has reason to think that the general public has not adopted the views of most of your critics. I saw a good review in the *Western Mail* and another in a Bradford paper, which is quite sensible and friendly.

He talked to me seriously also of my affairs. This is the psychological moment when, he thinks, we ought to get hold of all the copyrights and work them ourselves to the best advantage according to a plan he has in his head. In the later contracts (Methuen & Dent) he has introduced clauses which enable me to resume my rights on easy terms. The people we will have to deal with at a disadvantage are Heinemann and Fisher Unwin. With the first he does not anticipate any trouble. But Unwin will be the devil! Altogether he thinks that a thousand pounds will be the outside cost of the transactions if attacked at once.[5] Unfortunately I haven't the money and neither has he, and this is a business one can't go to a cold capitalist with; though it might be true, as Pink says, that there is practically no risk and that the amount would be repaid in three years with adequate interest. He is very confident as to that, but he didn't go actually into figures with me. I didn't ask him to do so, as the only likely person is . . . and I have made up my mind not to ask him—for reasons which I need not set down here. So the thing will have to be put off till I make some surplus money, and *that* is not likely to

(5) The difficulties referred to were that *Almayer's Folly* was the absolute property of Fisher Unwin, and *The Nigger of the "Narcissus"* of Heinemann.

be very soon. And by then the price will have gone up automatically and the affair will be still more difficult to carry through. Damnable position! However I have no millionaire friend and there is no help for it. I won't allow this disappointment or difficulty to spoil my holiday. We depart on Saturday evening 8.40 from L'pool Street Station via Hamburg—Berlin.

Give me news of yourself soon.

Yours ever,

J. Conrad.

P. S. Here is the address in Poland.

J. Conrad, c/o Mme. E. Zubrzycka.

Goszcza.

p. Slomniki.

Govt of Kielce,

Russian Poland.

Do let me know how you are and what you are doing.

[Capel House,]
Wednesday, [24th February, 1915.]

Dear Curle,

This is to tell you that we shall be at the Norfolk Hotel, Surrey Street,[1] on Friday evening. Will you look us up.

Yours ever,
J. CONRAD.

---

(1) Conrad and his family had now safely returned from Poland. It was at this hotel he invariably stayed, during these years, when in London.

The Norfolk Hotel,
Surrey Street,
Strand, W. C.
Friday, 5th Mch. [1915]

My dear Richard,

Robertson has behaved like the very Angel
of Civility. I am certain he will do what he can for Linton
Hope.[1]

We leave here to-morrow morning I think.
Courtney has scolded me bitterly in a column of the *Dly
Tel'ph*,[2] but I am not upset. Still I am going home with
that flea in my ear.

Drop us a card to Capel. Jessie and John[3]
send their love. So do I.

Yours ever,
J. CONRAD.

---

(1) My friend, J. M. Robertson, who was then one of the Under
Secretaries of State, had succeeded in getting for Linton Hope—
the brother of Conrad's very old friend, G. F. W. Hope—a post to
do with the examination of sea-planes.

(2) No doubt this refers to a review of *Within the Tides* written by W. L. Courtney in the *Daily Telegraph*.

(3) His wife and younger son.

Capel House,
Orlestone,
nr. Ashford.
20 Ap. '15.

Dear Richard,

Just a line to tell you that Linton Hope has got just the job he wanted as insp^{or} of sea-planes.[1] He's infinitely grateful to you for your introduction to Robertson, who seems a very efficient big gun indeed.

L. Hope has written at once to thank Roberts: and as he has not your address has asked me to convey his thanks to you. I also have written to Robertson.[2]

I can't write a line—damn it! Our love to you.

Yours,
J. C.

---

(1) and (2) See previous letter and note (1).

Capel House,
Orlestone,
nr. Ashford.
Wednesday, [May, 1915.]

My dear Curle,

Thanks for your letter. I couldn't reply at once because of a bad wrist which has been bothering me and hindering my work.

Re Ford. As you know we wanted something at once. A very shabby cheap Ford turning up for sale in Ashford I bought it, for the position was impossible.

We would be very glad if Mrs. Wedgwood[1] would fix some day next week. Jessie'll write to her to-morrow.

I cut short this missive, not feeling very well.

Yours ever,

J. CONRAD.

---

(1) Now Lady Wedgwood, the wife of Sir Ralph Wedgwood, my fellow executor and trustee of Conrad's will.

Capel House,
Orlestone,
nr. Ashford.
26 May '15.

Cher Seigneur,

Most decidedly! We shall be charmed to see you here any time.

I have been but indifferently well all this time —and now am quite seedy with lumbago.

Herewith, mon très cher, the book of *Victory* 1st U. S. Ed. but hardly the equivalent of a presentation copy. You shall have that in due course[1] for your noble shelves.

We have been thinking a good deal of you. Collective love.

Yours,
J. C.

---

(1) See note (1) to letter of July 22nd, 1914.

[Capel House.]
15 July 15.

Dear Curle,

So sorry I must put you off. I am nothing so far on with my work as I expected, and I must resolutely put away all temptation to dally with friends, (*dear* friends), by the way.

And I am somewhat gouty. I don't want to waste your week-end leave[1] on a preoccupied and irritable man. I don't for a moment suppose you'll take offence. You understand my view of our relations too well for that.

Yours far from happy,
J. CONRAD.

Shall write you before many days.

---

(1) From the Royal Naval. Volunteer Reserve.

[Capel House.]
Tuesday, [22nd September, 1915.]

Dear Richard,

Yes dear! Come along.

I've instructed Methuen to forward you a copy to Beauf^t Mans.—a copy of *Victory*, I mean.

Borys[1] left home yesterday at 11 a.m. to join the A.S.C. (M.T.) at Grove Park Depot as 2 lieut. We had a letter from him to-day. The details'll keep till you come to us on Sunday.

Yours ever,
J. CONRAD.

(1) Conrad's elder son, who had just joined the Army.

Capel House,
Orlestone,
nr. Ashford.
7 Oct. '15.

My dear Curle,

We are coming up to-morrow (Friday) to the Norfolk about 12. I shall probably lunch with Pinker.

Would you do me the kindness of securing 2 dress-circle seats for "Rom. and Juliet" to-morrow (Friday) night.[1] The 2 end seats on the *left* side of any row. If no dress circle obtainable in that position, then pray get two *stalls*. Jessie can not sit out a performance but in the end seat on the left of any row.[2]

She means to take John to Mask. and Cooke at 3. But I shall be at your disposal if you are free in the afternoon. Send us a tel. message to the Norfolk in the course of the morning about the tickets and other things that may occur to you. Jess would like to call on Mrs. Wedgwood on Sunday. On Monday, early, we go home.

Yours ever,

J. CONRAD.

(1) I accompanied Conrad and his wife to this performance.

(2) This was due to her injured knee.

Capel House,
Orlestone,
nr. Ashford.
18 Dec. 15.

My dear Richard,

We are very sorry to hear you had to retire to a Nursing Home again. You have taken an unlucky walk with John that afternoon.

Jessie does not write herself to-day as she's not feeling very well. I finished the story yesterday about 11 a.m.[1] Looked at as a whole it isn't bad. I laboured hard at the last; and I feel unexpectedly well (for me) now it is all over.

I trust your doctor is a man of sense and knowledge, and that one may believe what he says. Whatever you do, guard against those optimistic imprudences for which one pays by relapses.

We expect Borys on Monday on 48 hours' leave. He has been laid up with shingles for 3 days lately.

Our kindest regards,

Yours ever,
JPH CONRAD.

P.S. Please drop us a p.c. frequently. We want to know how you are getting on.

---

(1) I think this refers to *The Shadow Line.*

[Capel House.]
Saturday, [12th February, 1916.]

My dear Richard,

MS. received.[1] I haven't begun reading it yet, as I haven't quite finished writing my own stuff. Do it on Monday, I hope. If I see that my journey to Lond. can't come off soon I shall write to . . .[2] in a way to produce the desired effect.

Delighted to hear good news of your health.

Yours ever,

J. C.

(1) The MS. of my new volume of stories, *The Echo of Voices*.

(2) A publisher whom Conrad hoped to interest in the above volume.

Capel House,
Orlestone,
nr. Ashford.
22 Feb. '16.

My dear Richard,

I will talk to you at length about the stories[1] when you are well enough to come down here for a week-end.

My great concern just now is *how* to write something that would really influence . . .[2] To find the right thing to say. I would have preferred to see him. However I shall do it to-morrow or next day.

A consideration occurs to me whether spring would be a good time to publish the vol? You see there may be great events in the spring—favourable no doubt; but in any case distracting to the public mind. Whereas later in the year (say Sept.) the emotional state may have settled down somewhat. Reflect on this seriously. Yours indeed is delicate work. The value of these tales lies in the "nuances" of colour, of half-light; and in almost evanescent tremor of emotions. The vol: I am afraid won't have enough weight to resound unless the atmosphere is pretty still all around when it falls from the press. But don't mistake me! I like it very much. It interested me greatly. I haven't been able so far to hit upon the notion of a general title. Sorry. Dam' difficult thing to do for stuff of that very peculiar quality. I myself can hardly define the flavour. But Lord! What the publishers will make of it, God only knows.

Our love to you,   Ever yours,
J. CONRAD.

(1) and (2) See notes to previous letter.

[Capel House.]
Saturday, [4th March, 1916.]

Dear Richard,

I've had a very friendly answer from . . .[1]
Ask him on the telephone early on Monday if you can
see him in the afternoon of that day. Tuesday is barred
by . . . 's letter to me. So if Monday is impracticable you
had better suggest Friday afternoon for the interview so
as not to interfere with your Wed. and Thurs. visit to us
—see? Leaving here on Thurs. at 10.15 (Ashford) you
will be up in good time even to take him out for a cheap
lunch if you like. He is the sort of man for such sim-
plicities. A sympathetic sentimentalist. The personal interview is his own suggestion of course. He knows something of you, having read two of your books. He doesn't
say which. This literally *all* he says on the point.
The letter is friendly—very—in tone. But that, you
know, means nothing; and a sentimentalist on guard
against sentiment is the very devil to deal with in such
business. Give me a Philister any time.

Our love to you,

Ever yours,

J. CONRAD.

P.S. We had a letter from B.[2]—from Dunkirk, I guess,
or thereabouts. The men, gunners and transport are over
safely—through Dover route. But guns and cars dispatched by Avonmouth won't reach them for a week
or more yet.

(1) See note (2) to letter of February 12th.

(2) His son Borys.

Capel House,
Orlestone,
nr. Ashford.
29 Mch. '16.

My dear Curle,

Glad to hear you are getting on, but dam' sorry about the . . . fiasco.[1] Perfectly idiotic. Of course as mere business it could not have been a great thing, but the risk was not great and I thought the man had some feeling.

Directly the weather improves and steadies we hope to see you here. Just now you mustn't chance the journey since chills are what you must guard against. We'll talk of many things—and I have a little book for your Conrad Coll^on—unless D'day has sent it to you already. I haven't heard from Quinn[2] yet, but may reasonably expect something by the next mail.

Millais[3] is still at home—ailing. His service days are over I fear. We had a cheery letter from B. on Monday. Boy Robert[4] is going to the Worcester[5]—definitely.

Yours ever,

J. CONRAD.

---

(1) This publisher did not produce the book, which was published by Knopf in America.

(2) John Quinn, the great American collector of Conrad MSS.

(3) Sir John Millais, grandson of the painter, who was in the Navy.

(4) A son of Norman Douglas, the writer, whom the Conrads were helping to educate.

(5) The training-ship for the Merchant Service, where Borys Conrad was educated.

Capel House,
Orlestone,
nr. Ashford.
12 Ap. '16.

Très Cher,

I had a letter this morning from an American woman (elderly miss, I should think) reader of my works and collector of 1st ed^{ons}. She says she thinks she has got everything except the No. of the *Ox: and Cam: Rev: with* "Prince Roman," which is being hunted for, and the pamphlet preface to *N. of the N.* the price of which (she says) is more than she can afford. This last statement is interesting. I haven't the slightest intention to send it to her; but I feel half inclined to tell Saxton[1] I have 35 copies and ask him to get some New York dealer to make me an offer of £50 for them.[2] Qu'en pensez-vous? I really do want the money; and this, from what I hear, seems to me the psychological moment for working the American side.

I am up but behaving with the greatest prudence, keeping mostly upstairs till the weather takes a turn.

Ever yours,
JOSEPH CONRAD.

---

(1) A then member of the editorial staff of Doubleday, Page.

(2) This pamphlet is now worth about $75 a copy!

Capel House,
Orlestone,
nr. Ashford.
Tuesday, [April, 1916.]

My dear Curle,

Herewith a couple of cards to see my bust[1] if you feel like it.

I won't be able to come up. I haven't been well at all lately and don't like to risk a journey.

Pray don't think I would be hurt if you didn't go. This forwarding of the cards is just a geste d'amitié on my part to you. Nothing more.

Yours ever,

J. CONRAD.

---

(1) This, I think, must refer to the bust by J. Davidson, the American sculptor.

My dear Richard,

Mrs. Marwood[1] appreciated infinitely the sympathy of your letter. I am so glad you did write. Poor M. was buried on Wed. I was not in a state to attend.

W. Rothenstein's exhibition of portraits at the Leicester Gall. will open on Wed. next. Do look in please and let me have your opinion of my head which you will find there. I like it much. If your opinion is favourable too I shall try to get D'day, Page to use it for portrait to the Coll^d Ed^on in U.S.[2]

Yes. Do come when you are ready.

Yours,

J. C.

(1) I had written her a letter of condolence about her husband's death. He was a neighbour of the Conrads when they lived at Orleston, and Conrad used to see him every week and discuss literature and politics with him. Marwood had a most brilliant intellect, and his death was certainly a great blow to Conrad.

(2) A portrait head of Conrad by Rothenstein did appear as frontispiece to *The Secret Agent* in the Concord Edition published by Doubleday, Page in 1923. I do not know whether it is the same portrait as the one Conrad refers to here.

Capel House,
Orlestone,
nr. Ashford.
20 Augt. 16.

My dear Curle,

We were glad to hear from you. We hope you
are now settled down and improving in your health
rapidly.[1]

Of public affairs I have nothing to say that
you don't know already by the cables. Borys wishes in his
last letter to be remembered to you. He's still with the
guns being now att^d *personally* to the artillery of the
IIId corps. I suppose he is as much in the actual scrim-
mage as an officer of his corps can possibly be.

I will confess to you that I miss you considerably. Your departure, following on M'wood's death,
left a great void.[2] Our life here has been running in its
usual groove, but I am sorry to say Jessie has not been so
well as she is usually. John flourishes and keeps you in
mind. Gibbon[3] returned from Russia a week ago and without seeing us proceeded to Switzerland to seek the
bosom of his "petite famille." Millais[4] is invalided out
of the Navy for good. He and his mother made
friendly inquiries as to your health. We made the

---

(1) I had been sent to Africa.

(2) See note (1) to previous letter.

(3) Perceval Gibbon, the novelist, who was a friend of Conrad.

(4) Sir John Millais. See note (3) to letter of March 29. He died
not very long after.

acquaintance of a new young woman. She comes from Arizona and (strange to say!) she has an European mind. She is seeking to get herself adopted as our big daughter and is succeeding fairly. To put it shortly she's quite yum-yum. But those matters can't interest a man of your austere character. So I hasten away from these pretty frivolities to inform you that we had here Lord Northcliffe[5] for a Sunday afternoon. He was an immense success with John and Robert. In about 15 minutes they became extremely familiar with him, dragging him all over the place to look at birds' nests and so on. In return for these attentions, he invited them for two days to his house in Broadstairs. They are going there soon in the great man's Rolls-Royce which will come for them. That same subtle Northcliffe got round the Lady Jessie by feeling references to his mother, which certainly had the stamp of sincerity on them.

I suspect that you keep my letters and may some day deliver them to the printer's devil. Yes Sir! That's so! Not that I don't believe you to be a Perfect Gentleman—but isn't it written (in the correspondence of the Apostles, I believe) that "literary communications corrupt good manners"? I shall leave my impressions for viva voce on your return.

Retinger's[6] activities go on at white heat—personal success immense, political what it can be and indeed, better than one would have thought it possible in

---

(5) Lord Northcliffe was a great admirer of Conrad's genius, and as his country house was not far distant from Conrad's he used to go over occasionally.

(6) A Polish friend of Conrad.

the hopeless state of the Polish question. He created for himself certain titles to a hearing by accomplishing a brilliant piece of work last month as an unofficial intermediary between the Br. and Fr. Governments. In truth the position was delicate. But its too long a story for this letter. I too have dipped my fingers in diplomacy by writing a memorandum on the peace settlement on the Eastern front[6] which got into the F.O.[7] The official I interviewed later said as I was leaving—"Well, I never thought I would have this sort of conversation with the author of *The Nigger of the 'Narcissus.'* " Which shows the man to have the sense of contrasts in him, though he looked like a stick of sealing wax and seemed to be made of parchment. For the rest, a perfect homme du monde and some years ago (I understand) known for his succès de salon— of the non-political kind. Well—I must stop now—the continuation in my next.

Affect[te] regards from us all.

Yours ever,

J. Conrad.

---

(6) This, I imagine, must be "A Note on the Polish Problem" in *Notes on Life and Letters.*

(7) The Foreign Office.

Capel House
Orlestone,
nr. Ashford,
27. 3. '17.

Dear Richard,

This is only to tell you that your copy of
The Shadow Line[1] has been put aside here—till better
days.

For the rest, I am still like a man in a nightmare. And who can be articulate in a nightmare?[2] Borys
had a 10 days' leave from the front. He was impatient to
get back to his guns. Enfin!

I simply *can't* write.

Yours toujours,

J. CONRAD.

We are very lonely here. No one down for months and
months.

---

(1) It was published in 1917.

(2) As the War went on Conrad was more and more affected by it.

4. C. Hyde Park Mansions,
Marylebone Rd., N. W.
2d Dec. '17.

My dear Richard,

We are at this address for 3 months so that
Jessie should be treated for her unlucky knee joint. Of
late she was fairly in the way of becoming a cripple for
the rest of her days. Something has to be done.

We had news of the success of the operation;
and we send you here our affectionate congratulations on
your final escape from the disease[1] which has hung on to
you so long.

I had a lot of worry and anxiety of late,
about Jessie of course, and also other things. Such days
have to be lived through. As to news—well! All one's
interior and private life is knocked into a cocked hat
every morning by the public news, of which you know as
much as I do.

As 13 years ago, when Jessie was going to be
operated, *Nostromo*[2] is coming out. History repeats itself.
Only I hope that this time *N.* won't be the black frost he
was at his first appearance. I wrote a short preface "très
intime."

But all these things seem to have no importance now. One can't imagine a single human being likely
to be the least bit interested in such matters. Unless perhaps you! And so I have preserved most carefully *for you*
the corrected (first) proof of the New Edition where you

---

(1) Too optimistic: I had several internal operations in Africa.

(2) The new edition of *Nostromo* was published in 1918.

will be able to see at a glance all the corrections and the few changes I have felt myself compelled to make. Some of them do bear on the very passages you quote in your book on me.

This you must pardon me. I thought a great deal about you before making them. Of course the changes are merely verbal and affect no more than a dozen words.[3] Moreover I think you'll approve—in the end.

It's late. I am tired and nervous and chilly. So—"au revoir," for the present. Jessie sends her love.

Yours ever,
J. CONRAD.

---

(3) There were considerably more than a dozen.

Capel House,
Orlestone,
nr. Ashford.
Oct. 9th, 1918.

My dear Richard,

My last letter to you, I have every reason to think, has been submarined and I was just preparing to try my luck again when yours of 14/8/18 arrived. I am very glad of the generally good news you send me.

I am dictating this because I have a crippled right wrist. Gout has been clinging to my various limbs ever since the beginning of this year, practically.[1] I am going now to repeat to you in an abridged form the news contained in the drowned letter.

Early this year we spent some time in London on account of Jessie's knee. The surgeons put the limb in splints of a particular kind and assigned a three months' period to observe the result of that truly infernal-looking implement. It brought instant relief; and though the beastly affair weighed nearly six pounds she managed to go about a good deal with Borys who was on leave just then. Those two racketted together for a fortnight, dined in a club with Mrs. Wedgwood, who was charming to them both, visited theatres undeterred by the numerous air-raids and generally had a good time. I had gout. Then B. returned to France to be involved in the 3rd Army's mess and we went back to Capel to await developments. It was a horribly trying time.

---

(1) Conrad had been a victim to gout ever since his illness on the Congo in the early 'nineties.

The developments not being favourable (except in so far that I managed to finish a novel—*The Arrow of Gold*—on the 14th of June) we proceeded to town at once for further advice; the upshot of which was that a very big, if not exactly dangerous, operation on the knee[2] was performed by Sir Robert Jones[3] with apparent success. Borys fresh from the disastrous retreat, through which he had pulled out his battery entire after a lot of rear-guard fighting, obtained a special leave for the operation, and was a source of great comfort to me, not to speak of his mother. She having her two boys with her preserved a wonderful cheerfulness through it all. At the end of six weeks in a nursing home I took her back to Capel; but unluckily various small complications set in and now we are again in town for a fortnight, the prey of the surgeons. However I am assured on all hands that the ultimate success is certain. The bones have grown together, I am told; and considering that the joint has been in a horrible condition for upwards of fourteen years the slight setback after the operation is not to be wondered at. Yesterday she has actually put her foot to the ground and walked a few steps in her room in the nursing home, for the first time in more than three months.

The present disposition of the family forces is as follows: Mr. and Mrs. J. Conrad are going to retreat to Capel House next week, according to plans. Lt. B. Conrad is advancing in Flanders with the 2nd army and

---

(2) One of many similar operations that Mrs. Conrad had had.

(3) The famous Liverpool orthopaedic surgeon, who became a close personal friend of both Conrad and his wife.

is much bucked up. Master John Conrad is interned in a
preparatory school in Surrey for his third term and is
now reconciled to his horrible situation. I can't tell you
very much about further operations, beyond the fact that
they include a frontal attack upon *The Rescue*, which was
indeed begun some time ago but, I am sorry to say, has
been pushed feebly and has died out for a time. However,
in the present more favourable circumstances it shall be
taken up with vigour and is expected to achieve a success
by January next at the latest.

These are all the news up to date from my
front.

Rest assured, my dear Richard, that I re-
turn with the greatest warmth your regard and affection.
You too are often in our thoughts. During the anxious
passages of the last ten months I have more than once
missed your unfailing and friendly support. We both look
forward impatiently to seeing you again. I am getting on
—I mean in years. After sixty, one begins to count the
days, and gout, however faithful, is not a cheerful com-
panion. I am getting awfully crippled and it's about time
Jessie ceased to be so. And if that happens I don't really
mind very much if I have to end my days in a wheeled
chair like Macaulay's Lord Holland.[4] He kept his wits
to the end and I have the advantage over him that my wife
is not a Lady Holland. But one wants to have all one's
friends within reach.

I am delighted to hear of the travel book.[5]

(4) A character of whom Conrad was very fond of talking.
(5) *Wanderings*, published in 1920. It was dedicated to Conrad.

Perhaps you remember that I was always rather enthusiastic over that work. I wonder whether you changed in any way its plan and its tone. We shall see. I am warned that there is very little space left, so I will end here abruptly with love from Jessie and myself.

Ever yours,

J. CONRAD.

Spring Grove,
Wye, Kent.
25th May, '19.

My dear Curle,

Just a word of welcome[1] from a bed of sickness, I've had a most awful time ever since Jan^y.

I've just finished *The Rescue!*[2]

Of course, my dear fellow, you must come to see us as soon as you can spare the time.

My poor wife has to contemplate the delightful prospect of another operation in about three months' time.

I've here a set of privately prin^d booklets (of various things of mine) for you, also a 1st Ed. copy of *Shadow Line* and the complete first set corrected proofs of the new ed^{on} of *Nostromo*. All that may prove to you that you have not been forgotten.

Au revoir then. Drop us a line.

Yours always,
J. CONRAD.

---

(1) On my return from Africa.
(2) It was published in 1920.

[Spring Grove, Wye.]
Thursday, [19th June, 1919.]

Très cher Ami,

I have shown B. your letter. He was getting
too wretched at his unattached state and no prospect of
even some try in any direction. He has been immensely
cheered, and, I assure you, he is properly appreciative
of your friendly earnestness in the matter.[1] So are his
Mother and Father. We shall expect you next week as
you suggest and then I'll tell you all about my business
journey to town, and of my arrangements as to the disposal of the money amounting to about £3,080 *nett.*[2]

I am glad to see the *Arrow* has pleased you.
I am not at all sure of a good reception here. The sales
in America are, I understand, a good deal better than
Chance's or *Victory's.*

I am considerably better. How long it will last
no one can tell. Pink. told me he had seen you. He feels
very friendly toward you.

Jessie's love,

Ever yours,
J. CONRAD.

P. S. We shall be truly glad to see the Wedgwoods here
any time they feel inclined to run out.

---

(1) I was trying to get Borys employment.
(2) This refers to a capital sum he had been paid for the cinema
rights of some of his books.

[Spring Grove, Wye.]
Friday, [28th June, 1919.]

Dear Richard,

You are very good. Both I and B. agree absolutely with your view that this matter should be negotiated personally and *not* by letter.[1]

Please catch the 11 a.m. from Char. X tomorrow (Sat.). We will meet you at Ashford.

Edmund Candler[2] is coming by the same train to stay till Sunday.

Yours ever,
J. C.

---

(1) See note (1) to previous letter.
(2) The author and war correspondent.

Spring Grove, Wye.
7. July, '19.

My dear Curle,

Many thanks for your letter and for all the trouble you are taking about B's future and my own affairs.[1] The question of your health is very much in my mind. Do take care of yourself as far as it lies in your power.

On Friday next we proceed to Essex.[2] We will be back here on Sunday evening. Miss H. M. H. Capes[3] arrives for a 2-3 days' stay on Monday afternoon. The next week-end is clear.

Ever yours,

J. C.

P. S. Jessie sends her love. Drop her a line if you are coming.

The no. of Nth Am^{an} *Review* awaits you here. It was concealed inside the damned armchair.

---

(1) See two previous letters and notes.

(2) To visit the Hopes.

(3) An old friend of the Conrads, sister of Bernard Capes, the novelist.

Spring Grove,
Wye.
Tuesday, [8th July, 1919.]

My dear Curle,

I opened the enclosed letter by mistake.
Sorry.

I have yours of yesterday enclosing Knothe's[1]
to you.

Of course he must be immensely busy. In this
connection should he not see his way to place B. under
his own eye, perhaps he could recommend him to some
motor mf^g firm for employment or training—with
premium or otherwise. I feel that Knothe's word would
give the boy some standing under any circumstances.

I've just written you to say we will be away
this week-end. The *next* is clear, and·we hope to see you
here say on Friday ev^g (dinner) if that suits you.

Ever yours,
J. C.

(1) Col. Knothe, who was interesting himself on Borys's behalf.

Spring Grove,
Wye.
16. 7. '19.

My dear Curle,

We shall expect you to come on Friday by the 4.30 train from Char. X. Will you come on to Wye and walk up? We have to go out in the afternoon on unexpected business and *may* not be back in time for the car to meet you. It will run down later for your suit case. In any case we'll not be very late. ½ hour on the outside.

Infinite thanks for your letter. The invitation to the W.[1] has been sent.

Au revoir,

Yours,
J. C.

---

(1) The Wedgwoods.

Spring Grove,
Wye.
Monday, 4 Augst, 1919.

Dearest Curle,

Thanks for your good letter. To know of your readiness to stand by me at the critical time is a great comfort.[1]

B. had a most kind and promising answer from Col. Knothe[2]—making an appointment in B'ham[3] for the 14th. He answered it at once. But last night he got up suddenly a high temperature—and God only knows what may come of it. The Doctor has just left. We must wait and see. It may be a mere touch of malaria only. I am rather worried, the more so that John too has come back from school with a beastly cough, and is quite out of sorts. I am keeping well—for me. Pray let us know how *you* get on—in health of body and mind. Gardiner[4] was here and talked of you with most intelligent appreciation. The doctors have ordered him to California—poor fellow. Jessie sends her love.

Ever yours,
J. CONRAD.

P.S. *Arrow's* publication day 6th Augst.

---

(1) I suspect this refers to a promise by me to stay with him while his wife was being operated on.

(2) See letters and note of July 8th.

(3) Birmingham.

(4) Major Gordon Gardiner, whom Conrad had met in Scotland during the War. He recovered sufficiently to be able to stay in Europe.

Spring Grove, Wye.
24. 8. '19.

Dear Curle,

I think I wrote you already of B's reception
by K. He was most kind. The programme is for B. to de-
vote a month to the study of a certain chemical test (for
metals) and then join the Oldbury works, to learn metal-
testing by actual practice—with the promise of a post at
the end of 12 months—more or less.[1]

Nothing could be more satisfactory.

B. will try to get a coach in London so as to
be near us when J. is operated. Then at about 10 Oct. he
expects to proceed to Bir'gham.

Our warmest thanks for your interest and
effective agency in this affair. I sent a copy of *A. of G.*
to Mrs. Iris,[2] and Jessie wrote her a letter of thanks.

Have you seen this cutting? It has been re-
produced in several provincial papers.

Jessie sends her love. B. is now in Mull—
shooting. We shall be in London on the 28th for the examination, but intend to go home the same day. Jess.
would like to put off oper[on] (if any) till after we shifted
houses.[3] I'll keep you informed. We are most grateful to
you, my dear Richard, for your friendly offer.

Ever yours,

J. CONRAD.

(1) As a matter of fact, nothing came of all this.

(2) Conrad's name for Lady Wedgwood.

(3) The Conrads were about to move to Oswalds, Bishopsbourne,
near Canterbury. They had only taken Spring Grove, furnished, on
a short lease.

Spring Grove, Wye. 30. 8. '19.

My dear Curle,

Jessie has been considerably upset by the examination. She has been put to bed with a bad pulse for 3 days and asks me to thank you warmly for your good letter and tell you of the result at once.

Another operation is necessary. Sir R. Jones, who is very confident as to ultimate success, is going to the U. S. middle Sep^t and does not wish to operate till his return—that is about middle of Nov^{er}—as he has made up his mind to attend to the case himself throughout. He has asked me to bring Jessie to L'pool where he will be able to have her under his eye all the time.

From the domestic point of view the delay is not an unmixed evil as we'll be able to settle down (in a certain measure) in our new house[1] before going to L'pool in Nov. But it is a beastly prospect to live with and a charming Xmas tide to look forward to for both of us.

We are glad to know you are having a good time. I will write to you again soon. Directly you come south again you must come to see us—here if before the 20th Sept. or in the new house about the 15 Oct.—the first visitor no doubt.

Jessie sends her love and thanks.

Ever yours,

J. CONRAD.

P.S. Remember us affect^{ly} to the Gen. and Mrs. Wedgwood. We hope that John[2] is making a good recovery.

---

(1) Oswalds.   (2) The Wedgwoods' son.

Oswalds,
Bishopsbourne,
Kent.
15. 10. 19.

Dearest Richard,

I just sent off a letter to you c/o Pink. Now I know again your address I hasten to thank you for your letter received to-day; you are a very good friend, and we are both very grateful to you for your promise to stand by us in L'pool.[1]

Your better news about yourself has cheered me up. We are camped here with a few sticks of furniture, without curtains and carpets, and, in our state of horrid suspense, not caring to undertake anything more. Next spring I hope we will take steps to settle down to a comparatively civilized life.

Of course *you* may come if you care to run the risk. Let us know directly you return from Scotland.

All luck to you, my dear fellow, whenever you go and whatever you attempt. We'll discuss the pamph[ts][2] when we meet.

Jessie's love.

Ever yours,
J. CONRAD.

---

(1) Liverpool.

(2) No doubt some pamphlets containing his work which he thought of issuing.

Oswalds,
Bishopsbourne,
Kent.
11. 11. 19.

Dearest Dick:

Thanks for your good letter. I am very pleased with what you say of your plans for settling down.[1] It will be good for you I feel sure, and outside my household you are the person about whom I am most concerned both in thought and feelings.

I am going on with the play.[2] Vernon[3] was here yesterday.

Love.

Yours,
J. CONRAD.

P.S. Have you the *Rev. des Deux Mondes* with the article on *A. of G.?*

---

(1) I was planning a move into the country.
(2) *The Secret Agent.*
(3) A producer of plays.

Oswalds,
Bishopsbourne,
Kent.
12. 11. '19.
9.30 a.m.

Dearest Richard,

Thanks for yours. I did not hear from Wise,[1] but you may perhaps clinch that bargain in the sense of your letter—which is full of common-sense. The money is already spent.

I haven't the slightest recollection of the article "Books."[2] I am glad you found my "Anatole." Do keep a list of your discoveries in view of a vol. by and bye.[3]

I have finished Act Two of the play[4] (2 scenes) and shall in a moment begin Act Three. A great adventure!

In haste. Love.   Yours,
                          J. C.

P.S. On second thoughts I'll drop a line to Wise. But you may drop a note to him too. Thanks, dear Dick, for all your kindly offices.

---

(1) T. J. Wise, the famous bibliophile, who had begun to collect Conrad.

(2) Conrad had very little memory about the different articles he had written on various occasions. When I was collecting the material for *Notes on Life and Letters* several times I discovered articles by him in old periodicals which, until his memory was jogged, he actually denied having written. On the other hand, he had a marvellous memory for the books he had read and the incidents of his life.

(3) *Notes on Life and Letters* was published in 1921.

(4) See previous letter and note (2).

Oswalds,
Bishopsbourne,
Kent.
Saturday, [22nd November, 1919.]

My dear Curle,

We are coming to London on Thursday on our way to L'pool for the operation,[1] which is fixed for Tuesday, 2d of Dec.

I can't tell you where we will be staying. But I'll send you a wire on Wednesday. We shall proceed to L'pool on Sunday noon, as Jessie's room at the Nurs. Home won't be vacant till that day.

On Thurs. I'll be most likely lunching with Heinemann and having tea with an American. But we could meet in the evening. On Friday I lunch with Vernon (Vedrenne's partner) who is to be the producer of the play. I have just finished Act III. I shan't touch the IV till the worry is over and we are settled down in L'pool.

Our love,

Yours,

J. CONRAD.

P.S. The Archbishop's wife[2] called yesterday. This is fame! Unfortunately Jessie was in bed and not well enough to see her.

P.P.S. This is good news about the Travels[3] being in the press.

---

(1) Mrs. Conrad's knee was operated upon at this time by Sir Robert Jones.

(2) Mrs. Davidson, wife of the Archbishop of Canterbury.

(3) The references is to my book, *Wanderings*.

85 Kingsley Rd.,
L'pool.
12. 12. 19.

Dearest Richard,

I snatch a moment for this scrawl. Everything is going on so well that Jessie may be released from the Home about the 22d—in which case we should spend only one day in London. I'll let you know the exact date.

Of course I feel happy. But as to doing anything it is impossible here. All the time is taken up in going up and down this dratted town for one thing or another and sitting with Jessie. My mind is a blank. I can't even look through the $R.$[1] proofs.

I won't call on your tried friendship to come over here. Jessie sends her love and her thanks for your sympathy. All this seems too good to be true and I have a dread of some beastly development. But every one assures me that it isn't likely. The wound itself is healing beautifully.

We shall want, of course, to see you on our passage through. Will you be in town?

Ever aff^ctly yours,
J. C.

---

(1) *The Rescue.*

[Liverpool]
Wedy, [26th December, 1919.]

Dearest Curle,

We'll be at the Norfolk. Jessie arrives about 4 o'clock. If you come about 7 you will find me there too.

We are very, very glad at your plans for settling down.[1]

We'll have a good long talk.

Yours,

J. C.

---

(1) I was then taking a house in Oxfordshire.

Oswalds,
Bishopsbourne,
Kent.

Dearest Dick,
Tuesday, [Jan. 1920]

Ever so many thanks for your letter of yesterday inclosing the list of papers for the misce[ous] volume.[1] It seems to me absolutely complete. I don't think there can be a scrap of my writing hiding anywhere. There is nothing I can remember, at any rate.[2]

The questions you raise require a little thinking over; I want to consult you about my ideas on that matter.[3] I will write to you soon, very soon, asking you to run down here. Just now the conditions are unspeakable—rather. I have been unable to work or even to think.

It is true I wrote two prefaces in my life, one for Ada Gals. the other for Edward Garnett's book.[4] But they were not concerned with their work. In one I speak of Maupassant *only*—in the other of Turgeniev, almost exclusively. But writing for your book would have been another matter altogether. It would have had to be a direct personal appreciation. You see the difference?

---

(1) *Notes on Life and Letters.*

(2) Conrad's memory was at fault. He overlooked the Galsworthy article, which was subsequently published in *Last Essays.*

(3) The question of whether he would write an introduction to my *Wanderings,* which I had suggested to him.

(4) Conrad wrote prefaces for Mrs. John Galsworthy's volume of translations from Maupassant and for Edward Garnett's book on Turgeniev.

The facts of our case:—you the author of the only serious Study of J. C. (a book well known and generally acknowledged); the actual dedication staring people in the face—would have thrown a complexion of complimentary futility upon the most sincere expression of literary opinion and personal regard.

All this may be controverted, no doubt,—but I shrank from the risk, both for your sake and mine. It did not seem to me worth the occasion. On general grounds a laudatory preface is not a good thing. The critics react instinctively. No, I don't think it would be good for the book. Honestly I don't. It looks as if the author had not enough faith in himself. And in this instance there is a disadvantage that in a book of that sort (travel) there is no question of sheer art involved which could be taken up and treated in a preface abstractedly. It must be either personal backing up—or nothing. A most difficult thing to do and moreover extremely liable to defeat its own ends. It occurs to me, however, that the dedication might be cancelled and, in that case, I would—if you really want it—try to write you a letter which you could print. I would try—and that's all I can say.[5] And even then I fear you would have to wait for it. My dear, I am unable just now to write prefaces for my own stuff! They are clamouring for them in U. S. I can't even tackle the text of the *Resc.* My mental state is awful.

Ever yours,

J. CONRAD.

(5) I did not cancel my dedication to Conrad and on the strength of this letter abandoned my request to him for an introduction. He subsequently wrote an introduction to my book, *Into the East.*

Oswalds,
Bishopsbourne,
Kent.
Jan. 19th, 1920.

Dearest Richard,

I am too slack and languid to sit up to the table and write with pen and ink. I am not too feeble to talk, however, and if you feel at all disposed perhaps you would run down on Wednesday to lunch and sleep.

I can't ask you for a few days because I am now engaged in correcting the text of *The Rescue,* which I promised the publishers in England and America would be ready end of Jany. As I have done nothing to it till the last three days Miss H.[1] and I are slaving at it all the morning and often in the afternoon in order to get through somewhere near the promised date.

It would do me good to see you, morally and intellectually, and I hope you won't mind coming for such a short time. We will have a good long talk. Pray drop us a line by return. Jessie's love.

Ever yours,
J. CONRAD.

---

(1) Miss Hallowes, Conrad's secretary.

Oswalds,
Bishopsbourne,
Kent.
26.2.20.

Dearest Dick,

I was glad to get a word from you.

We expect to see you on Sat. for week-end by the 4.55 Vic. Carola[1] arrives to-morrow.

Revision of *Resc.* finished 2 days ago in bed. But I am up now and feeling better.

We'll have some talk and I want to hear how it stands with the pub^{on} of your book. My affair with H. L^d Ed^{on}[2] is settled. 1000 sets.

More viva voce.

Regards from all.

Yours,
J. C.

---

(1) A Polish cousin of Conrad's. She and her sister were his two closest relatives.

(2) The limited edition of his works which Heinemann published. The number printed was actually 780.

Oswalds,
Bishopsbourne,
Kent.
March 12th, 1920.

My dear Richard,

Sorry the visit didn't come off. Better luck
next time; and if there is a genuine desire of the third
party you may fix a date next week, if you like.

Books arrived this moment. Many thanks for
the affectionately inscribed copies, and the note of ages
is interesting.[1] I will talk to you about the two works
with perfect and even offensive sincerity when we meet.
My wrist is bad again. I am not anxious to write; and
of dictating I swear to you I got enough with that ass
Verloc and his tragic wife.[2] That, however, will be done
with by next Monday, unless there is a special curse on
me of which I know nothing—as yet!

Jessie has taken a turn for the better.

All our love.

Yours,

J. CONRAD.

---

(1) I think I sent him at this time copies of my first book, *Aspects
of George Meredith,* and of my latest volume of short stories, *The
Echo of Voices.*

(2) The reference is to his drama, *The Secret Agent.*

Oswalds,
Bishopsbourne,
Kent.
March 18th. 1920.

My dear Curle,

Yes, next week will do, if you make it Friday. Saturday won't because the shover[1] departs for week end for amorous reasons.

I enclose you here a letter from . . .[2] Do you think that what he means is that 500 dollars has been asked for *one* pamphlet?

Well! It is a startling bit of information, to be sure, if it is as I take it. I don't understand why . . . should be indignant at 500 dollars being asked for a 10 set, since he has already paid $50 for single copies.

I have answered . . . rather sharply, not liking quite that suggestion that I should "prevent" . . . Prevent what? How can I stop the dealers asking what they jolly well like. That little word "prevent" raised my dander considerably.

The first draft of the Play[3] was finished on the 15th. I am now working at it, inking my fingers and ruffling my hair during the usual agonies. It is truly a damnable job, but to be candid with you it isn't so bad this time—at any rate as yet. It's when I tackle the draft of the Third Act that the tug-of-war will come.

It is arranged that Vernon will come here some

(1) His nickname for his chauffeur.
(2) A Conrad collector in the U. S. A.
(3) *The Secret Agent.*

day after April 6th. I hear he is now busy rehearsing the next piece to be produced on the 6th. It may very well be that mine will follow; which would bring my production somewhere to the end of May. But devil only knows!

Aubry[4] is going to translate, and our intention is to throw the thing at the pigeons in the Théâtre du Vieux Colombier. We may of course have it thrown back at us. Pigeons are wily birds.

Jessie sends her love. She spends her days in the chair now—upstairs. But really there is no change— and what we are most concerned at is the depressing effect of it on her. She worries herself with gloomy forebodings.

Altogether life is pretty hard. Bills still come in—naturally. The grave is the only refuge from them.

Ever yours,
J. CONRAD.

---

(4) G. Jean-Aubry, the author and editor of the official *Life and Letters* of Conrad.

Oswalds,
Bishopsbourne,
Kent.
23.8.20.

My dear Richard,

Thanks for you[rs.] The car will meet the train on Friday, 12.42.

Can't ask you to stop for week-end because Jessie is still laid up and the servants are going on leave. There is also trouble with the pump, which will cause, I am afraid, 2 days' interruption of hot water supply when the repairs are taken in hand. The man may not turn up till Friday. Awfully sorry; but there are a good many of us and 2 girls will have their hands full. Also the cooking will be chancy, as Dora will have to try her hand at it on Sund. You had better not risk it.

I am glad your book[1] is to be looked out for any day now. I am very impatient. Inscribe the copy to both of us, as J. will appreciate very much being associated in the presentation of the Vol.

All luck to it—and to you in every way.
Au revoir then,

Yours ever,
J. CONRAD.

P.S. A full set of *corrected* galley slips of *Resc.* is awaiting your instructions to forward or keep.

---

(1) *Wanderings.*

Oswalds,
Bishopsbourne,
Kent.
Thursday, 25.3.20.

Dear Richard,

Just a line to thank you for the book.

As I turn the pages my consideration for you grows to the proportions of respect.

There is a beauty of easy moving prose—charm of phrase—felicity of words which give the strongest possible impression of mastery of language and individual vision of things and men.

My warmest congratulations.[1]

Au revoir to-morrow.

Yours,

J. CONRAD.

---

(1) Letters such as this should not be taken too seriously. When Conrad praised the work of his friends he was sometimes more lavish than critical.

Oswalds,
Bishopsbourne,
Kent.
8.4.20.

My dear Curle,

I'll be writing soon to you to ask you to come—but this week-end is impossible.

Jessie sends her love. She's beginning to look more like herself.

Did I tell you I had a wire from Quinn apparently just to tell me he had P.[1] to lunch—and to acknowledge a few pp. of MS. I sent him.

Plumber's and drainage bill fell on my head this morning—also enormous coal acc^t. I am still reeling from the blow.

Hein^{nn} was here for lunch yesterday. It will have to be 750 sets I think. Some booksellers told his man that if 750 they will take 10 sets, but if 1,000 only three! However Hein^{nn} has enough paper for the greater num^{er}.[2] Pink returns on Tuesday.

I am still gouty in hand and foot but I manage to crawl about. Miss H. returns from leave to-day, and to-morrow I will try to start work.

Jessie's love. Mine too.

Yours,

J. Conrad.

Impt. I want to know what sort of reviews is your book getting? The more I look at it, the more I think of it. But these reviewers are so superficial! I am quite anxious. Give me your impression.

---

(1) J. B. Pinker.

(2) Refers to the collected edition of his works.

Oswalds,
Bishopsbourne,
Kent.
5 May. 20.

My dear Curle,

Jessie was operated on Sat. last at home under local anesth^c. A 4 inch cut down to the bone and involving a nerve. She had a most awful time of it with pain all Sunday and Mond^y. She is a little easier now. The worst of it is that all the trouble has not been removed. There is another inflamed region which will have to be treated—probably by an operation of a more serious nature. But not yet. Sir R. Jones will come again, I suppose next week.

There being a Nurse in the house I must ask you to come only on Sat. ev^g instead of Friday—unless untoward developments take place; in which case I shall wire you to Coleherne Court on Fr^y or Sat^y morn^g to stop you. But that is not likely.

I don't feel very bright, as you may imagine. Jessie sends her love.

Always yours,
J. CONRAD.

Oswalds,
Bishopsbourne,
Kent.
Sat. 15. 5. '20.

Dearest Richard,

Sir R. J.[1] is just gone after declaring himself pleased with the general improvement in the state of the limb. The trouble tends to become localised in one spot, but the appearances were not definite enough as yet to venture on an incision. So nothing was done except a very thorough examination, and Sir R. will come again to see Jessie either this week or the next—according to the report our local surgeon is to send him in a few days.

Meantime hot fomentations and complete immobility in the long chair in which poor Jessie has been lying now night and day for 3 weeks. She is very cheerful and sends affectionate messages to yourself.

I had to put off Pink's visit till next Friday. There are no news of anything stirring in my affairs. I like your travel book more and more both as personal expression and as individual prose—writing of a fascinating quality. (I can get no prose of any kind out of myself.)

Yours ever,

J. CONRAD.

(1) Sir Robert Jones, the surgeon.

Oswalds,
Bishopsbourne,
Kent.
24. 5. 20.

My dear Richard,

      I won't conceal from you that I am much affected by your last two letters.[1] I can't contemplate your possible departure for India with equanimity. But you alone can judge of the proper conduct of *your* life. I can only feel that your decision is bound to affect *mine* intimately with a sense of loss in its deeper values. That much I had to say—tho' I daresay it is no news to you. For the rest—perhaps! Yes, perhaps it would be better for you to get away for a time. The great consideration is that such a move is bound to affect the complexion of your whole future. That is unavoidable. On the other hand, the pressure of the material necessities may be irresistible in this case. I am thinking of all this with great and, I believe, quite unselfish anxiety.

      Walpole[2] has asked permission to come down on the 5th—for the week-end. If you want to meet him this is an opportunity.

      Enough for this time. Our love.

Yours,

J. CONRAD.

(1) In which I had announced my intention of going to Burma for a time.

(2) Hugh Walpole, the novelist. It was then that I made his acquaintance.

Oswalds,
Bishopsbourne,
Kent.
2 June, '20.

My dear Curle,

I will have to be out all day Saturday, and for this reason and also for another connected with the servants we must ask you to come only on Sunday by the morning train—the one that arrives at Cant^y East at 12.24 and will be met either by our car or Sneller's taxi. Awfully sorry to keep you off for a day, but there has been a lot of complications—of the domestic order.

I don't think much of the temporary Editorship.[1] If you go out you will stick out there I fear. However!

Au revoir then on Sunday, for I hope you'll be not so offended by this letter as to refuse to come.

Love from us all.

Yours ever,
J. CONRAD.

---

(1) My editorship of the *Rangoon Times*. I only held it for four months, though the owner wanted me to stay for five years.

Oswalds,
Bishopsbourne,
Kent.
June 14th. 1920.

My dear Curle,

The announcement of the actual date is quite
a shock.[1] You must know that after a very good afternoon
in the B.M.[2] I returned home feeling very well and with
most pleasant recollections of the day with you and
Walpole, ended by profitable reading, but during the
night a severe attack of gout came in the right wrist,
which, notwithstanding my efforts to re-act, laid me flat on
my back in considerable pain and, what is worse, an ex-
treme lowness of spirits. On Wednesday we heard that Sir
R. J. had decided to put off his visit for a week or more
in consequence of the report from the local surgeon and
partly owing to the pressing nature of his engagements
for the past week. Of course he could have done nothing
if he had come. How it was that I did not write to you on
Wednesday evening you will guess. Just then I was not
in a state to remember anything of what I had to do.
Of course I might have asked Miss H. to drop you a line,
but I repeat again that I was not in a state to do anything.

As the attack was sharp so the recovery may
be quick. I am certainly better now, but I don't know

(1) Of my departure for Burma.

(2) I think Conrad had gone to the British Museum to look up
some books to help him with facts either for *The Rover* or for
Suspense.

whether it will be at all possible for me to travel up to town on Thursday. And then there will be this consideration, that Sir R. J. may select that particular day for coming down here. Upon the whole I think the prospect is hopeless, and yet I would like very much to do it. I understand quite well that your time is bound to be taken up by final arrangements for your departure and your prolonged absence from England, but really, my dear Richard, it is no use speculating on what *I* may be able to do. It would be much more to the purpose, from my point of view, to ask you direct—what are *you* able to do? Can you come down on Saturday and stay over Sunday, or perhaps (to save every hour of the first working day) you would go back to town on Sunday night.

Please drop me a line at once and also let me know where you will be staying in London so that, in case of developments of any kind, I may write or wire you in town. No more at present because even dictating requires a big effort.

Yours always,
J. CONRAD.

Oswalds,
Bishopsbourne,
Kent.
Tuesday, [22nd June, 1920.]

My dear Richard,

Thanks for your letter of farewell. This is only to wish you, from us all, Godspeed and the best of luck.

I will write to you c/o *Rang. Times* in a fortnight, and give you general news of the house. I am most grateful to you for all the arrangements you've made for my vol. of coll^{ed} pieces.[1]

Whether I'll still be here to greet you in the spring I don't know; but I want you to take with you the assurance of my great regard for the writer and of my deep and constant affection for the man.

Yours always,
JOSEPH CONRAD.

---

(1) *Notes on Life and Letters.* I had recently been gathering together for him the material for this volume.

Oswalds,
Bishopsbourne,
Kent.
18. 8. 20

Dearest Richard,

I had two letters from you, one from P^t Said
and 3 days ago one from Colombo—and I thought of you
reposing under the shadow of Adam's Peak in the Garden Island of the tropics.

Things here are pretty well. Jessie is having another try at resuming walking exercise. Sir Robert
went away yesterday very pleased with the state of affairs,
tho' not quite certain whether another incision will not
have to be made in a month's time. But we all hope that
the patch of pain will subside gradually under a course
of massage. On the 1st of Sep^t we are going to Deal where
I have taken "a suite" in a hotel for three weeks—while
Miss H. departs (to the Lakes [?]) on her holiday. I shall
busy myself there with the text of *Notes on Life & Letters*
vol., which we have decided to fling out to the public next
spring. The Nap^{ic} novel is in its 3 chap^t.[1] All very lame
and unsatisfactory—so far.

John works two hours per day and seems
anxious as to his comm. entrance exam. for Tonbridge.
The cricket week[2] was attended by immense crowds. We
had nobody but Ralph[3] staying with us. I did not go once.

But I went to lunch with Lady Northcote at

(1) *Suspense.*

(2) The famous Canterbury "Cricket Week."

(3) Younger son of J. B. Pinker.

Eastwell Park. The Duchess of Albany[4] was there and
also Lady Gwendolen Cecil—and *she* was very interesting
and friendly. But the other too was very good, full of
sense and sympathy in her talk about the European
situation. Altogether a very pleasant experience. B. was
invited too and drove me over.

Next event was T. J. W.[5] turning up for
lunch and holding us spellbound by the flow of his utter-
ance. A very friendly person indeed—got on with Jessie
very well. So did old Dent,[6] who came with his son for one
night and looked most venerable sitting in the big gilded
armchair in his black coat which showed off his white
beard, while his child (Hugh D) sang to us Elizabethan
love songs. Très chic. Afterwards General Gunter—but
that is a long story which may be told later—in the next
dispatch.

B's laid up with a beastly bad throat. Karola[7]
has departed for Italy. I make her an allowance of £130
p.y. for 2 years certain with Pink's approval. That same
P. was 3 days with us, enjoying—as he said—my pros-
perity and planning ways and means to sustain all this
splendour.

I am spending more than I ought to—and I
am constitutionally unable to put on the brakes, unless in
such a manner as to smash everything. You know what I
mean—because you *do* know me.

---

(4) Daughter-in-law of Queen Victoria.

(5) T. J. Wise, the book collector.

(6) His publisher.

(7) One of Conrad's Polish cousins.

John is working quite hard (for him), that is about 3 hrs. p. day. There has turned up a prospect of a very good post for B. in connection with Richborough, which has been bought from the Gov^t by the firm of Alvan Richards (£6,000,000). B. just now is laid up with a very nasty throat and is in great trouble about it. However the thing is by no means certain and anyhow looks much too good to be true—as it were.

There was no one here during the first part of Aug^st. Walp.[8] is in Cornwall. Pinker is the only one who came for the night; and my oldest friend, G. F. W. Hope,[9] is just gone (23^d Aug.) after spending the week-end with us.

On the *first of Sept.* we are all going to Deal for 3 weeks. We will go by car which I intend to keep there during our stay. The dist^ce from here is only 19 miles, but the change for Jessie will be considerable all the same. Nurse goes with us of course. While we are there I will try to pull together the text of the vol of *Notes on Life & Letters* and also write a cinema scenario of "Gaspar Ruiz."[10] I am ashamed to tell you this—but one must live! Pinker himself is coming over to help me with it! I fancy he had the offer of a large sum from some good quarter for a Conrad scenario.

If one is to condescend to that sort of thing, well then, all considered, I prefer Cinema to Stage. The

---

(8) Hugh Walpole.

(9) Conrad had known him since the early '80s.

(10) This was written in conjunction with J. B. Pinker, but has never been produced.

Movie is just a silly stunt for silly people—but the theatre
is more compromising since it is capable of falsifying the
very soul of one's work both on the imaginative and on the
intellectual side—besides having some sort of inferior
poetics of its own which is bound to play havoc with that
imponderable quality of creative literary expression which
depends on one's individuality.[11]

I don't write this in the way of excuse for my
villainy. I believe that I am right in what I've said. I will
stop short here—to be continued in my next in about a
month's time. Love from my wife and the boys.

Always yours most affectionately,

JOSEPH CONRAD.

[Finished] *23 Aug^t*.

---

(11) Conrad always expressed the greatest contempt for the
stage.

Oswalds,
Bishopsbourne,
Kent.
9. 10. 20. 1 o'clock.

My dear Richard,

While awaiting the arrival of Doubleday[1] ("with my son Nelson") who are coming to-day by road to lunch and may be here any moment, I begin this letter to you. And I am very sorry to confess that it is only my second.

I am, my dear fellow, treating you badly, very badly. But I am too old to change my spots—and anyhow animals of my sort never do.

I have this morning (in fact about 10 minutes ago) finished my last preface (or Au'rs Note) for the volume of collected pieces. It will appear (1st Ed.) next spring. While revising the text you were very vividly with me—your friendship, your kindness, your personality, and I missed more than ever your voice, your characteristic turn of conversation, the downrightness of your mind and the warm genuineness of your feelings. I arranged finally the order of the papers on the list in your own hand-writing you made for me quite a long time ago. After some tentative shiftings the order remains practically as you wrote it down—with the addition of course of the 3 *D. Mail* pieces which were not on your list and of the short article on my flight.[2]

---

(1) F. N. Doubleday, his American publisher.

(2) Refers to *Notes on Life and Letters*. See letter of June 22, 1920 and note.

We spent 3 weeks in Deal to give poor Jessie a change. After our return here (on the 21st Sept.) she went on improving in her walking powers till a few days ago when she had to go to bed again with a new development of her old pereostitis. She is getting quite sick of these ups and downs. Still the pain has subsided since and she will attempt to-day to come down to lunch.

As to me, I feel a depression of spirits against which I can and do react—up to now. My novel is hung up for the present.[3] I am writing a cinema play based on "Gaspar Ruiz"—I mean *I*, myself, am doing it—and Laskers[4] Co. is interested in my efforts. It will be done next week—as to the rough draft, from which I shall dictate an extended scenario to Miss H. Lasker's "literary editor" (Heavens!) is in London. He will read it first (and pay for the privilege) and if approved of the thing will go to the "Continuity Writer" (did you ever hear of such an animal?), while another payment will go into my pocket and make it bulge out. At least Pinker says so. He comes frequently over here and is actually (and effectively) assisting me in this performance, which seems as futile and insecure as walking on a tight rope—and at bottom much less dignified.

The sensation of the moment in this household is that Norman McKinnel asked for the play and after reading it 'phoned to P.'s office asking about terms.[5]

What happened afterwards is just at present

---

(3) Probably *Suspense*.

(4) No doubt a mistake for Lasky.

(5) Nothing came of this.

"wropt in mystery." But that, as you know, is Pinker's way. I am not worrying myself. In the States Belasco asked to see it—but he has *not* telephoned, I believe.

Those are the news. Apart from that: Walpole has been here and inquired tenderly after you. He [is] very pleased with the reception of his new novel, *The Captives*. It is a very good "Walpole," a little larger in conception and in treatment.

I wish to goodness *you* would write a novel! Edward[6] was here for two nights and a day.

Doubleday and his son Nelson paid their visit. He is apparently pleased with the prospects of my work in America and very confident as to its permanent (paying) value. Obviously there is a sale; but the advance of *Rescue* on the *Arrow* (so far) is insignificant (if any), notwithstanding their high hopes. As to the coll[ed] Edition in the States, it is now finally fixed at 750 sets—and through P.'s efforts a payment of $12,000 has been secured. Here the death of Heinemann makes no difference. You will be interested to hear that the whole Ed[on] is subscribed. Print and paper are very good.

I trust nothing will delay your return next spring. John is to try for Tonbridge on the 15 Nov[er]. If he passes he will go there on the 20 Jan[y], 21. I am still in hopes to arrange to take Jessie to Corsica for Fbr. Mch. and Ap. Ajaccio is a good wintering place. If we are there when you pass through the Med[an] you must land in Marseilles and come over (one night's passage) to us for a week. But all my plans are doubtful and my hopes are

(6) Edward Garnett.

faint. Poor Millais died—at last![7] Lady M. is heartbroken. Colvin is very, very shaky.[8] You are much in our thoughts —never doubt that.

Ever affectionately yours,

JOSEPH CONRAD.

(7) Sir John Millais, Bart. The Millais were neighbours of the Conrads when they lived at Orlestone.

(8) Sir Sidney Colvin. He survived till 1927.

Oswalds,
Bishopsbourne,
Kent.
Monday. 22d. Nov. 1920.
6. p. m.

My dear Richard,

We were much distressed by the news of your illness. I am sorry you discovered the realism of my hospital scenes at your own cost.[1] Still there are worse places than tropical hospitals. I wonder if your cruise in the pilot-brig[2] will set you up sufficiently for the trip up country. I am awaiting with anxiety your next letter, if only a few words just to tell us how you are getting on.

Jessie is gone to-day to town for a week. This news will give you the measure of her improvement in general. In particular it means that she can walk about the house with both crutches with some facility and that she can get in and out of the car without too much trouble. My mind about her is much more at ease than it has been for the last 2 years and she herself is quite hopeful as to the future. Sir Robert will see her on Thursday in London and I will run up on that day to hear his verdict and then I'll proceed to Burys Court (Pinker) for the week-end.

We have had a most glorious dry weather

(1) I had had an attack of dengue fever and was laid up in the Rangoon Hospital. In writing to Conrad about it I had said that it reminded me of the description, in *Lord Jim*, of the hospital in Singapore.

(2) After leaving the hospital I had gone to stay with the pilots in their brig, which lay about twenty-four miles out at sea from the mouth of the Rangoon River.

since 1st Sepr. The last few days there was frost in the morning, all the slope of the Park being white till about 10 o'clock.

Did I tell you that I've finished all my Author's notes? I have even written the one for the vol. of *Life and Letters* (next March). They are also to be pub^d in book form 250 cop. in Eng^d and as many in the U. S. I will keep a copy for you. It will of course bring me a little money, about £180 for the Eng^{sh} e^d and quite £200 for the U. S. set. Every little bit counts. Money runs out like water! I am quite nervous. I *don't* get on with the novel.[3]

The actual piece of news for this letter bears upon the play. (*Secret Agent.*) Norman McKinnel has definitely accepted it.[4] He is now making his financial arrangements and intends to make it his *second* production. I would have preferred it to be the first. However! But the actor is good—he believes in the thing—he will no doubt put his back into the part (Mr. Verloc), and so I have accepted these conditions. Nothing is signed yet tho'.

I have finished the film-play of "G. Ruiz" ("The Strong Man"),[5] but as to its actual fate, Borys' prospects of entering a wireless manufacturing establishm. (experimental work and inventions) and John's success in his entr^{ce} exam. for Tonbridge, these will be told you in my next.

(3) Probably *Suspense*.

(4) See letter and note (5) of October 9th, 1920.

(5) See letter and note (11) of August 18th, 1920.

I can't shake off the feeling of anxiety about you. I do hope it will occur to you to write soon. Mrs. Iris has been asking for news of you. Jessie is seeing her to-day. I can't tell you how delighted and excited I am at what you say about the post in London which will enable you to settle in Eng^d. Can't you tell me what it is? I am a discreet person.

All our loves.

Ever most affect^ly yours

JOSEPH CONRAD.

Oswalds,
Bishopsbourne,
Kent.

My very dear Richard,   22.1.21.

Your letter was just in time to catch us before our departure to Corsica.[1]

John has been deposited at Tonbridge and I do hope will be happy there. We are leaving (with the car) to-morrow at 8.30—for Calais, Amiens, Rouen, Orleans, Moulins, Valence, Marseille—Ajaccio, and the weather is by no means promising.

Borys wil. take us as far as Rouen, making a detour to Amiens [and] Albert to see a little of the Somme front. At Rouen he will leave us and go back to Mortlake where he has a berth with a wireless appliances Man'g Co. directed by Dr. Mackintosh—a very old friend of ours. B. is very keen on this opening.

Jessie trots about—with one crutch—quite smartly. The only worry is a persistent pain area which we can't get rid of yet. She sends you her affecte regards, in which all here join.

We will be in Ajaccio (Hotel Continental) till the 20th Ap. for certain. Will you be able to push a point that way on your homeward journey? I am glad you had such an interesting time and still more glad to know of your good health and spirits.

Au revoir, cher—here or in Corsica.

Ever affectly yours,

JOSEPH CONRAD.

(1) Conrad, accompanied by his wife and the Pinkers, stayed for a month or more in Corsica.

Oswalds,
Bishopsbourne,
Kent.
9. 6. '21.

Dear Richard,

Our love and welcome to you.[1] Yes. Certainly next week will do. Will you come on Friday 17th for lunch. Car will meet you.

9.15 a.m. from Vic. gets Cant[ry] 11.20 and the next good train is 3 p.m. from Char. X gets to C. at 5.4.

Pray drop us a line.

Ever yours,
J. CONRAD.

---

(1) On my return from the East.

Oswalds,
Bishopsbourne,
Kent.
27. 7. '21.

Dear Dick,

What has become of you? Drop us a line to say you are well.

Am leaving for P's[1] to-day and shall be back on Friday evening.

Our love.

Yours,
J. CONRAD.

---

(1) Pinker's house in Surrey.

Oswalds,
Bishopsbourne,
Kent.
Tuesday, 1st Aug. 1921.

Dearest Dick,

Most sorry we can't have you this week-end.
The whole Pinker family are staying here till the 8th.
Could you come on the 10th till the 12th evening?

Pray drop us a line.

Our love.

Yours,
J. C.

[Oswalds]
31 Augst 21.

Dear Dick,

The week-end after this next one will not do. But any day after Tuesday the 13th you will be welcome for a night's stay—or if not then the week-end of 17th (Sept.). Pray drop us a line. I am trying desperately to get on with the novel[1] and feel rather worried about it.

I am glad of your good news. Jessie joins me in love to you.

Yours,
J. CONRAD.

(1) Either *Suspense* or *The Rover*.

Oswalds,
Bishopsbourne,
Kent.
12. 9. '21.

My dear Curle,

In fixing your visit for this next week-end I had forgotten that my very old friend Hope's visit was booked for that date.[1]

That being so, would you prefer to come down here for a couple of nights in the course of this week?

If so please let us know by a p.-c. as soon as possible.

Otherwise we can put you up for the week-end, but it would be in the Nursery wing.

Yours affectly,
J. CONRAD.

(1) On this visit I made the acquaintance of G. F. W. Hope, Conrad's oldest friend.

[Oswalds.]
Weday 12. 10. 21.

Dear Richard,

Will you come on Sat. for lunch and week-end.
It was impossible to find out before what were Jessie's
plans.

Hope you are bright and chirpy.

Yours ever,

J. CONRAD.

P.S. Drop us a line.

Oswalds,
Bishopsbourne,
Kent,
Saturday, [5 Nov., 1921].

My dear Curle,

  I hoped to get back from Burys Court[1] to town last Monday and then see you. But I felt pretty bad in the morning and so went on with Jessie home in the car. Ever since I've been lame in the left hand and generally in the dumps.

  I've been thinking of you a lot tho'. During Jessie's stay in London there was a lot of people all the time in the rooms. As I remained only the Thursday evg. and the Friday morning I had to be in attendance. My absence would have been too marked. On Friday I lunched with Doubleday and left town at 4. It was an awful grind.

Ever yours,
J. Conrad.

P.S. Jessie just tells me that Mrs. Iris told her (on Sat.) that you had lumbago. If I had known I would have gone back to town on Monday anyhow. You may believe me. Give me a word of news.

---

(1) Pinker's home in Surrey.

Oswalds,
Bishopsbourne,
Kent,
12 Nov. '21.

Dearest Richard,

Pardon the delay in answering your last,
which made me feel a bit unhappy about you. The very
fact that I understand your feelings thoroughly makes it
difficult to write. You may feel sure of my understanding
and sympathy—but no words can be of any help in an
unhappiness so intimate; and my thoughts if I were to
set them out in their confused state would not be of any
use to you. This is not a matter for action. It is a
question of sheer endurance—a call not on your wisdom
(in which I believe) but on your character—in which I
have the greatest confidence. But that is comfort for me
—not for you.

In the matter of the preface, I have thought
it over and I regret not to be able to tell you more than
that I'll see what I can do.[1] I am very doubtful—not of
my wish but of my ability. I won't talk to you now of my
mental state. Send the MS. anyhow. I may find a way to
squeeze something out of myself. If affection alone could
do it you would not have to wait long.

Jessie sends her love and I am always most
[?] affectionately

Yours,

JOSEPH CONRAD.

---

(1) The Preface for my book, *Into the East*. Conrad finally wrote
it after about a year's delay due to finishing off *The Rover*.

Oswalds,
Bishopsbourne,
Kent,
Friday, [18th Nov., 1921.]

Dear Dick,

Can you, and do you care to, come down to-morrow by train arriving Cant^{ry} 5.4 or 6.18 to dine and stay over Sunday? Please wire.[1]

Yours,
J. C.

---

(1) Typical of many brief notes I had from Conrad.

[Oswalds.]
23. 11. '21.

Dear Dick,

Certainly—come for next week end arr^g on Sat. at 12.44. The car will meet—unless something unexpected prevents.

Could you look up Gordon Gardiner, 12 Queen Anne's Gate—in our name, so to speak. He has been rather seedy—but should he be able, bring him along if you can. You would not mind giving him up the best spare room?

Of course, this is only a suggestion.

Drop us a line.

Our love.

Yours,

J. CONRAD.

[Oswalds.]
16. 12. 21.

Dear Richard,

Perhaps I misdirected the short note I wrote some days ago proposing you should come to us on Saturday, 24th for dinner and stay till Wed^y morning.

Jessie however wants you to come on Sat. for *lunch* and I have wired you to-day to that effect. This confirms it. So we shall expect you then. Should the car not be there (par force majeure) you must take a taxi. But I'll try to get it there in time. Au revoir.

Ever yours,

J. Conrad.

Oswalds,
Bishopsbourne,
Kent,
Sat: 5 p.m., [February, 1922.]

My dear Curle,

So sorry I forgot to ask Miss H. to drop you a line of my safe arrival last night. I was ½ a day in bed just to rest. I have dictated a memo to Eric,[1] of which I send a carbon for you to see. Pray return. I think it is all right.

Au revoir soon. Our love.

Yours,

J. CONRAD.

---

(1) Eric Pinker, J. B. Pinker's eldest son.

[Oswalds.]
Monday, 6. p.m., [20th March, 1922.]

Dear Dick,

This letter came in the afternoon. Seeing my name on the envelope I opened it before I noticed that it was addressed to you. Sorry.

I have been working hard ever since you left the house, dictating in the morning, correcting all the rest of the time.

Ever yours,
J. C.

P.S. I will be coming by train on Thursday. Vic. 11.28. Therefore if you happen into the R.A.C.[1] you may find [me] there about noon.

---

(1) The Royal Automobile Club, of which Conrad was a member. He constantly went there when he was in London.

Oswalds,
Bishopsbourne,
Kent,
22. 3. 22.

Dear Dick,

Sir W.R.[1] not coming up to-morrow, I shall try to transact some business with Eric in the morning.

Ever so many thanks for the admirable memorandum.[2] I shall of course be guided by it.

I intend to lunch at the R.A.C. about 1.15 and remain there till you turn up.

But it *may* be possible that I should have to go [to] see E.P.[3] again in the afternoon. However it's unlikely.

I hope to get off by the 4.20.

Ever yours,
J. C.

---

(1) I am not sure to whom this refers.

(2) Refers, I fancy, to a memorandum about his finances that I had written for him.

(3) Eric Pinker.

[Oswalds.]
[5 April, 1922]

My dear Curle,

a) You may just as well say, which is a truth, that I do read biography and memoirs. History has a fascination for me. Naval, military, political.

b) Will that never be taken for granted? Do give it a rest in print.[1]

I am interested even in party politics, the develop. of institutions and opinions—and emotions of mankind in the mass. I feel deeply what happens in the world—a genuine sentiment qualified by irony—something like that.

Am laid up and in pain.

Ever yrs.

J. C.

---

(1) This letter refers to the proof of a little personal article on him which I had written for the *Daily Mail*. In it there was a remark of mine to the effect that he could not have written his books in any language but English.

Oswalds,
Bishopsbourne,
Kent,
April 24th. 1922.

My dear Richard,

  I did ask Jessie to express to you my intense satisfaction at your having obtained that post on the *Daily Mail.*[1] If it will leave you time enough to do your own work, I certainly think that the salary is not at all bad to begin with. May every possible success attend your work in the journalistic sphere. I shall be immensely interested to know what precisely you will have to do and whether you will be able to find some intimate satisfaction in your daily task.

  I have this morning received the article for the *Blue Peter.*[2] I think I have given you already to understand the nature of my feelings. Indeed, I spoke to you very openly, expressing my fundamental objection to the character you wished to give to it. I do not for a moment expect that what I am going to say here will convince you or influence you in the least. And, indeed, I have neither the wish nor the right to assert my position. I will only point out to you that my feelings in that matter are at least as legitimate as your own. It is a strange fate that everything that I have, of set artistic purpose, laboured to leave indefinite, suggestive, in the penumbra of initial

---

(1) I had just joined the staff of the *Daily Mail* as a leader writer.

(2) The following paragraphs refer to an article by me entitled "Joseph Conrad in the East."

inspiration, should have that light turned on to it and its insignificance (as compared with, I might say without megalomania, the ampleness of my conceptions) exposed for any fool to comment upon or even for average minds to be disappointed with. Didn't it ever occur to you, my dear Curle, that I knew what I was doing in leaving the facts of my life and even of my tales in the background? Explicitness, my dear fellow, is fatal to the glamour of all artistic work, robbing it of all suggestiveness, destroying all illusion. You seem to believe in literalness and explicitness, in facts and also in expression. Yet nothing is more clear than the utter insignificance of explicit statement and also its power to call attention away from things that matter in the region of art.

There, however, I am afraid we will never agree. Your praise of my work, allied to your analysis of its origins (which really are not its origins at all, as you know perfectly well), sounds exaggerated by the mere force of contrast. I wouldn't talk like this if I did not attach a very great value to everything you write about me and did not believe in its wide influence. It isn't a matter of literary criticism at all if I venture to point out to you that the dogmatic, ex-cathedra tone that you have adopted in your article positively frightens me. As you tell me that you have a copy of the article by you I'll venture to make a few alterations, more to let you see what is in my mind than with any hope of convincing you. I will only remark to you, my dear, that it is generally known that you are my intimate friend, that the text carries an air of authority and that a lot of dam-fools will ascribe to me the initiative and the sanction of all the

views and facts expressed. And one really could not blame
them if they thought and said that I must have wanted
all those facts disclosed.

All those are my personal feelings. You won't
wonder at them if I call your attention to the fact that in
"Youth," in which East or West are of no importance
whatever, I kept the name of the Port of landing out of
the record of "poeticised" sensations. The paragraph you
quote of the East meeting the narrator is all right in
itself; whereas directly it's connected with . . .[3] it becomes nothing at all . . . is a damned hole without any
beach and without any glamour, and in relation to the
parag. is not in tone. Therefore the par., when pinned to
a particular spot, must appear diminished—a fake. And
yet it is true!

However, those are all private feelings. I
think too that the impression of gloom, oppression, and
tragedy, is too much emphasised. You know, my dear, I
have suffered from such judgments in the early days; but
now the point of view, even in America, has swung in
another direction; and truly I don't believe myself that
my tales are gloomy, or even very tragic, that is not with
a pessimistic intention. Anyway, that reputation, whether
justified or not, has deprived me of innumerable readers
and I can only regret that you have found it necessary to
make it, as it were, the ground-tone of your laudatory
article.

One more suggestion. Perhaps you may find
it possible to shorten to a certain extent the quotations,

(3) I have here purposely omitted the name because Conrad was
very anxious that no one should know it, for the reasons he gives.

which are, of course, admirably selected. I think that for *Blue Peter* there would be too much text; in America it would, of course, not matter.

I have written lately to Eric telling him about your post, at the end of my letter, and just mentioning that you will be probably sending him an article on me which you would wish him to place in the U. S.

I have been again laid up, but I attempt to scrawl a little more. It is to ask you to consider the modifications I have suggested to your article p^t 1. After all your thought remains untouched, and they are not much in themselves.

Ever yours,
J. CONRAD.

Jessie sends her love.

[Oswalds.]
Sat. 10. A.M. [29th April, 1922]

Dearest Dick,

I was just going to write to you that I was perfectly satisfied, when your second letter arrived and has troubled me greatly. Why scrap a valuable piece of work?[1]

I respect your labour too much to remain unmoved by your proposal. You have I fear, my dear fellow, thought too much of what I have written. I am in the habit to be unreserved with you as to my feelings and opinions—but I can never feel *hostile* towards anything you do. I respect your point of view even if I do not totally agree. It is after all a question of more or less expediency.

Suppression would lie on my conscience—unless you have arrived at some personal conviction about it. My alterations could not have disgusted you to that extent. In p. 1 I have run my pen through 2 statements of fact—of quite minor importance—and slightly altered the wording in one or two cases. Also made a few verbal changes. In p[t] 2, apart from some slight verbal changes—not interfering with the spirit of your argument—I struck out the phrase in which the word *tragedian* occurs. It is

---

(1) What follows refers to my natural answer to his previous letter. It was typical of Conrad that, although he could be exasperated by the stupidity of a critic, nevertheless his desire not to hurt feelings soon got the upper hand. The article as finally corrected by me, incorporating some of his suggestions, met with Conrad's approval and was eventually published in the *Blue Peter*.

a repetition, but you have no idea with what force it comes to the ordinary reader! You have called me a poet more than once before and the word tragedy (or tragic) occurs also at least twice before. You are supposed to be the man who knows more about me than anybody else. Don't forget, my dear, that as a *selling* author my position is by no means assured in the U. S. yet; and the average mind shrinks from tragic issues.

  I had to write this before settling down to my dictating.

Yours with great affection,

J. Conrad.

[Oswalds.]
2 May '22.

My dear Richard,

I have just got your letter. If you do not object to my alterations, then publish the article in the form in which you have first conceived it.[1] And if you could work into it (since it is written for the man in the street) something about my work having the quality of interest—as the m-in-the-s understands it—the interest of surprise, of story etc., you will be rendering me a great service. I still suffer from the reputation of being a gloomy, depressing author.

I showed your letter to Jessie, who sends you her warm sympathy and suggests you should come down on Sat. for the week-end if you can manage. How do you feel about it, my dear fellow? Drop us a line.

Affctly yrs,
J. C.

(1) This refers to the article mentioned in the two previous letters.

[Oswalds]
Wed. 10. 5. 22.

Dearest Dick,

 We will be in London on Thursday for the night.

 Could you meet me at the R.A.C. at say *11.45*. At 12.45 I will have to go to Pinker's office and all my afternoon will be taken up with worrying negotiations.

 Article received.

 We start for Burys Court in an hour, and will spend the night there.

 If you can not be at R.A.C. as above please, dear R., send me a *wire* there.

     Ever yours,
     J. C.

Thursday. 6 p.m. [25th May, 1922]

Dearest Dick,

Come along for lunch, tho' I fear we won't be able to meet *that* train. The 6.18 p.m. we could meet.

Your proof has just arrived.[1]

I've been working a bit lately and will not "cut the vein" on account of your visit; but there will be plenty of time for talks.

Ever yours,
J. C.

---

(1) No doubt, proof of my *Blue Peter* article, "Joseph Conrad in the East," published in the September-October issue.

[Oswalds]
Sunday. 5.30. [2nd July, 1922.]

My dear Dick,

We are coming up on Tuesday, for a week or so. Cannot give you the name of hotel, but it will *not* be Brown's. May 'phone you on Tuesday, or rather ask B.[1] to do so, for he will know on Monday.

Our love to you,

J. CONRAD.

---

(1) His son, Borys.

[Oswalds]
Thursday. 29. 6. 22.

My dear Dick,

I expect to be in London next week (Mond. or Tuesd.) with the finished (but not quite revised) *Rover*. You may imagine in what mental state I am. The whole thing came on me at the last as through a broken dam. A month of constant tension of thought. Could hardly bear to speak to anybody—let alone write.

I feel I've to thank you for the sympathetic note on *With Conrad at Sea*[1]—that preposterous bosh. I am very grateful.

No more now. I am still at work and under the strain.

Ever yours,
J. C.

Jessie's love.

---

(1) This refers to a review I had written on a book entitled *With Joseph Conrad at Sea,* describing Conrad's trip in the North Sea during the War.

[Oswalds.]
24: 7: 22.

My dear Curle,

Thanks for your friendly letter.

B. was here this week-end. He showed me several communications from both sides of Daimler business (the Hire D. Co., London and the Daimler, Coventry) from which one can not but suppose that they mean to give him some sort of job. Firms don't write letters for a joke or simply to kill time.[1]

I have begun your Preface.[2] Done about 400 w. It will be finished this week for you to see. 2,000 w. minimum. I suppose that will do?

Let me know at once how I am to address Wedgwood. General—or what—on envelope and inside.[3]

Love from us both.

Yrs,

J. CONRAD.

---

(1) His son, Borys, got a job with Daimler's.

(2) Refers to the preface he wrote for my book, *Into the East*. It turned out to be more like 3,000 words in length.

(3) Sir Ralph Wedgwood became a brigadier-general during the War, but dropped the use of the rank afterwards.

[Oswalds.]
28. 8. 22.

My dear Dick,

      I am thinking of coming to town to-morrow and perhaps you will meet me at the train (11.30)—that is, if you do not get a wire early saying I am unable. I feel however pretty well so far and want to have a talk with you on one or two matters of importance.

      Jessie's love.

Yours,

J. C.

P.S. Should you be engaged, 'phone me a message at the R.A.C.[1] in the course of the morning.

---

(1) The Royal Automobile Club.

[Liverpool (¹)]
Sept. 18. Monday. [1922]

My dear R. C.

We will be at the Curzon Hotel about five to-morrow (Tuesday.)

I have been feeling far from bright all these days. Otherwise it was a good time.

Yours,

J. C.

---

(1) I think he had been, with his wife, to Liverpool as guests of Sir Robert Jones.

Oswalds,
Bishopsbourne,
Kent,

Dearest Dick,   1st Oct. '22.

I can't let the new month begin without asking how you are. In truth all at once I have become quite anxious about you. Do please drop us a line; a comprehensive line to tell us shortly of your "public" and "private" activities.

Are you going to invest in the *Dy. Mail* stock?

How is your health
   a) physical
   b) mental
   c) moral—by which I mean degree of depression or exaltation from which you may suffer.

We thought you may [might] have proposed yourself for this week-end.

Lady Millais[1] came to lunch on Friday and asked about you.

I have been doing nothing but thinking—absorbing myself in constant meditation—over the novel. It's almost there! Almost to be grasped. Almost ready to flow over on the paper—but not quite yet.[2] I am fighting off depression. A word from you would help. Our love.

Ever yours,
J. CONRAD.

P.S. I've given a year's notice to Bell!!![3] Am scared now.

(1) Daughter-in-law of Sir John Millais, the artist.

(2) Refers presumably to *Suspense*.

(3) Colonel Bell, the owner of Oswalds.

[Oswalds,]
Monday [16th October, 1922]

Dearest Dick,

I snatch this bit of paper to thank you hurriedly for your very welcome letter with the good news about the agreement. I think you have reason to be satisfied. The McM. imprint[1] has some value in itself.

I was in town last Wed., saw poor Hope[2] and had a long talk, then rushed home. I did not write to you because we were to meet at noon and we had none too much time till 4 p.m. to exchange our news.

Am coming next Wed. to lunch with Nettlefold, Benrimo and R. Thorndike of the Ambassador's Theatre. Afterwards we will go to a rough rehearsal.[3]

Would love to get a sight of you at noon in R.A.C. where I shall be till ¼ to one. After rehearsal I will go home, probably by the 6.12 Can. St. Jessie's love.

Ever yrs,

J. CONRAD.

P.S. Myriam Lewis is to act Mrs. Verloc.

---

(1) This paragraph refers to my agreement with Macmillan for the publication of my book, *Into the East*.

(2) His oldest friend, then an invalid.

(3) Of his play, *The Secret Agent*. The men mentioned in this paragraph were connected with the production.

Oswalds,
Bishopsbourne,
Kent.
[October or November, 1922]

Dearest Dick,

I wired you to-day: "Next Thursday."

I do not think that it would be feasible to arrange the visit to the theatre afterwards. I saw only Act One yesterday. They went through the motions with their parts in their hands. It *was* promising. M. Lewis will do. The boy playing Stevie is excellent!

What was most pleasant was the atmosphere of belief in the play and the evident anxiety to do their best for it.[1]

I am looking forward very much to the lunch. You know how I prize women's appreciation, which, for a man not specialising in sentiment, is about the greatest reward one's sincerity can obtain.[2]

Yours always,
J. CONRAD.

Suppose we lunch at one? I will have to leave you at 2.30 so as not to keep those people waiting. We could *meet* at 12.30.

---

(1) Refers to a rehearsal of *The Secret Agent* which he attended.

(2) I had asked him to meet a woman friend of mine at lunch.

Dearest Richard,

We were pleased to hear from you in that cheerful tone.

Jessie went to bed yesterday. It is not much —an internal chill—getting better to-day; but she will have to be careful as to exerting herself for a few days.

I am afraid next Sat. is an impossible day— or else nothing would please us more. The Camerons will be in and out all that day (both Sir M. and Lady C.) to look for some rooms in Birch'g'ton or R'gate to transport Miss Kinkaid to.[1] We promised to help with the car and they will sleep here. Vexing—but this is the sort of thing one can't put off.

The discussion in the papers goes on, the critics telling each other "You have made rather an ass of yourself," "Look at the fine drama that's in it," "What a shame," and things of that sort.

I feel that all this affair is perfectly asinine. The public was beginning to come after only one blank day.[2]

Really the only person that need not feel an ass is me. I tell you this in all modesty.

We must have you and . . . next week if it can be done.

In haste for post.   Ever affectly yours,

J. C.

Jessie's love.

---

(1) Miss Kinkaid was an artist to whose little catalogue of pictures Conrad wrote a preface.

(2) Refers to the taking off of *The Secret Agent* after only one week.

[Oswalds.]
[17th November, 1922.]

Dearest Dick,

I return the proof in which I pulled together the phrasing here and [there], but have altered nothing.

It arrived this morning and now at 5 p.m. after meditating over it I came to the conclusion that no addition (of the sort I myself contemplated for a moment) could be fitted in without looking suspect—or at any rate tactless, out of place—if it were to be more than the three lines inserted on the margin of the last page. And even that I leave to your judgment.

If you reject the insertion then take care to transfer the semi-colon after *tales* to after the word *earth*—when the page will read just as correctly as to punct^{on} as with the insert left in.[1]

Jessie is better. She sends her love.

I think next Sat. can be managed.

Ever affec^{tly} yrs,
J. C.

P.S. Yes, my dear, the pref. as you wish to offer it to me in pamph. form will fetch something which, especially now after the play-failure, would be of help.[2] I think the serial^{on} of *Rover* will have to be given up too.

---

(1) This letter refers to his preface for my book, *Into the East,* of which I had sent him a proof.

(2) Refers to the suggestion of mine—which I carried out—of printing a little private edition of Conrad's preface to my book.

[Oswalds.]
Tuesday. [5th December, 1922.]

My dear Dick,

I am coming up to-morrow Wed^y by the 9.53 to lunch with Doubleday at 1.30 and will be at the R.A.C. about noon.

It would be nice to get a sight of you, the more so as there are developments of which I could talk to you.

However it is not pressing desperately.
You might 'phone a message to R.A.C.
Love
Yours,
J. C.

Oswalds,
Bishopsbourne.
Dec. 8th. 1922.

My dear Curle,

I am sending you here now the case on which I should like to get the opinion of your tax recovery people. My case is very simple. All my income comes out of my inkstand, partly from royalties on old books and serial rights of new books, advances on royalties which mean large sums paid at once before the book actually earns them, and suchlike ways, which you will be just as well able to explain as myself. My income, except for a small part of it, comes to me irregularly, the amounts each year depending for their bulk on the dates of book-publications or the serial appearances. We may take the steady part of my income at £2,000 or a little less. As you know yourself there are years in which I publish no book, or a book of very small money value. In this current year, for instance, I have earned nothing, but have been assessed for tax and super-tax on the rendering of three very good years to the amount of nearly £1,800, which is really killing me completely.

All my monies coming from England and America have been for years passing through the hands of J. B. Pinker, who always made out my statement of income, after, I suppose, deducting his commission, (a variable quantity). I think that J. B. has always deducted £200 for my secretary's salary, and I believe managed some two years ago to make them admit the claim of about £300 or so for travelling expenses.

This, as far as I know, is the situation. I ask myself whether deduction is made of the interest I pay on monies which from time to time I owe to Pinker in the general process of his financing me through any given year. But I suppose it is so. Certain payments, like, for instance, for Edition de Luxe in 1921 which swelled the total receipts to £10,000 and only occurred once, have been treated as income and came into the average for assessing my income for 1922–3. The same thing happened in 1919, when payment of £1,200 for *Arrow's* serial rights was treated as income and swelled the average of the assessment for 1919–20. *The Rescue*, which earned nearly £3,000 serial rights, did the same for 1920–1.

This is the present situation.

I would also like to know what effect it would produce on my liability to tax and super-tax if I were to live in France; which I would do in any case, for my position is not good and two years economising abroad would put it right. Of course, if my taxation were reduced on account of me taking up my domicile in the South of France somewhere, it would certainly hasten the recovery and permit me to take up my domicile in England again. It is only sheer necessity which drives me to contemplate living abroad for at least nine months in the year for the next two years.[1]

Many thanks in advance for the trouble you are willing to take in this matter.   Ever yours,

J. Conrad.

---

(1) Conrad was so generous and open-handed that he was never really free from money troubles. Needless to say, he never settled in France.

[Oswalds.]
15th December 1922.

Dearest Dick,

I am (so is [are] Jessie and John) looking forward to your arrival—in just a week's time.[1]

God knows—I would like to know that your trouble, whatever it is, is off your shoulders—partly or entirely.

Our love to you.

Yours,
J. CONRAD.

(1) For Christmas.

[Oswalds]
Tuesday. 2. 1. 23.

Dearest Dick,

We were glad to get your note. I do hope all your worries will be "downed" for good soon.

Can you advise me how I could get hold of the No. of *New Review* for Sept^er 1897?[1] Would advertising in the literary press be the only way—and if so what papers?

B. was here last Sunday for a few hours. He was notified of a rise in his salary, amounting to £85, from Jan 1st (£100 less 15%). He thinks it is very good after only 4½ months service.—I had an optimistic letter from Eric about the prospect of *The Rover* being out *next* autumn.

Le Figaro has asked Aubry[2] for an article on Joseph Conrad at an early date. Boom in J. C. in France! Our dear love to you.

Ever yours
J. C.

---

(1) *The Nigger of the "Narcissus"* appeared serially in five numbers of this review. Conrad possessed the other four.

(2) G. Jean-Aubry, his French friend.

[Oswalds]
6 Jan. 23.

Dearest Dick,

Many thanks for the cheque for £60 received to-day—the product of the pamphlet and a most welcome windfall, which I owe to your ingenious friendship.[1] The hard times are beginning with a vengeance—but as long as I can go on with the novel[2] I will not be dismayed. I wish I were feeling better in myself—but I am going on since the first so far unchecked.

Jessie sends her love. I would be happy to hear some good news from you.

Ever yours,
J. CONRAD.

---

(1) See letter and note (2) of November 17, 1922.
(2) *Suspense*.

Oswalds
Friday. [2nd February, 1923.]

Dearest Dick,

I was glad to see from your letter to Jessie that you are all right and that you started working at your novel.[1] This is great news.

When are you coming down here? Will next week-end suit (I mean from Friday to Sund. morning)? I miss your company.

I am working—but nothing like the rate I ought to keep up to make things look better. And yet I am hard at it all the time. Can't talk about it on paper. No doubt the anxiety itself prevents me in a way to reach my best. I find life rather a trial just now. I am a little worried about B's health—and the more so because he is doing well otherwise.

Ever yrs,
J. C.

(1) Only finished in 1927!

138

text[Oswalds]
12 M'ch. '23.

Dearest Dick,

Pardon this scrap of paper. It is only to send you my congratulations on reaching the mature age of 40—and to thank you for the copy of the special edition received to-day.[1] I like the appearance very much. I hope the book will meet with the recognition it deserves.

I have begun to-day an introduction to a forthcoming biography of Crane by a man called Beer. He and Knopf came here on Thurs. last on that business—which is in truth a marvellously good business for me. I want to give him about 3,500 words.[2] It will take some doing, tho'.

I am sorry no end to see from Jessie's letter that you cannot come over with me into the Land of the Mohicans.[3] I have a short note from F.N.D.[4] (from the Bahamas). The letter in which I announced your *possible* arrival with me had not reached him yet when he wrote. He must have it now. He intends to be back long before the date of the voyage of the New Columbus (without Pinzon!!?).

Can't get up any enthusiasm for it. More details when we meet—which will have to be soon.

Ever yrs,

J. CONRAD.

(1) A copy of the large-paper edition of *Into the East*.

(2) The introduction worked out at about 8,000 words eventually.

(3) I had hoped to go with him to America.

(4) F. N. Doubleday.

Oswalds.
22. 3. 23.

Dearest Dick,

I hope things are going as well as possible with you. I am just finishing the Crane Introduction[1] and my head is simply buzzing with the strain.

Best wishes for the book's career begun yesterday—wasn't it?[2]

Ever yours,
J. CONRAD.

---

(1) See previous letter and note (2).
(2) *Into the East.*

[Oswalds.]
10 Ap. '23.

Dearest Dick,

As I see from your letter to Jessie that you mean, if you can, to see me off at Glesga I write to ask if you would have any objection to start from St. Pancras at 9.50 a.m. on Friday. arr. Glas. 7.5 p.m. I propose the Midland as the food on that line is eatable—but on the . . . is is *not*.[1]

Of course, if it is too early for you we might start at 12.15, arr. G. 9.25.

You are a dear fellow to stand by me so nobly. Methinks we might travel 3d on Midland and in fact spend most of our time in the restaurant car. What do you say?

Ever yours,
J. CONRAD.

B. came for a few hours last Sunday. Everything's very satis[ry] with him. Will you come to the Curzon on the 16th at 7.30 and dine?

---

(1) We travelled together to Glasgow by the Midland Railway, and I saw him off to New York the next morning from Greenock in the "Tuscania."

Oswalds,
Bishopsbourne,
Kent.
12 Ap. '23.

Dearest Dick,

I was just about to write to you specially on the Dole articles.[1] They are wonderfully the right thing: matter, tone, attitude, interest. They are in fact so easy and interesting that I (being myself in the "trade") am not a bit surprised at your feeling tired. Only real concentration could have produced such all round excellence.

Jessie is lost in admiration.

I'll tell you more of my feelings when we meet on Monday.

Sorry, my dear fellow, that I cannot toe the line on Wednesday. Absolutely impossible. Indeed I regret it very much.[2]

3 lines in your letter have taken a certain worry out of the back of my head. I did not know how much there was of it till the relief was felt about 30 minutes ago.

Ever yours
J. CONRAD.

---

(1) The first of some articles on the "Dole" which I contributed to the *Daily Mail*.

(2) I had wanted him to meet a friend of mine.

[Tuscania]
29. Ap. 23.

Dearest Dick,

It's the best I can do. It is very poor, but I trust you will be able to make something of it. I can not look these pages over.[1] We will be at the jetty on Tuesday 10 a.m. and I shall try to send them across to the outgoing mail boat which will leave at noon.

I have had a bad wrist (left) which hindered me in this work. It is distinctly better to-day, tho' painful. I have had a radio. from Doubleday. The passage was good and M. Bone[2] has been looking after me like a good fellow. Can't say I feel very bright. No need to tell Jessie that. You are very much in my thoughts and I feel I would give anything to have you by. Pardon me for not saying any more.

Ever yours,
J. CONRAD.

(1) Conrad had arranged to write an article on his way over to America for publication in the London *Evening News*. It was entitled "Ocean Travel," and he posted it to me as soon as he arrived.

(2) Muirhead Bone, the etcher, a brother of David Bone, the Captain of the "Tuscania."

This letter was written on the last page of the MS. of "Ocean Travel."

Effendi Hill,
Oyster Bay, Long Island,
New York,
11. 5. 23.

Dearest Dick,

Am awfully rushed or else lying prostrate to recover—but in either case in no writing mood. But I must drop you a line to say that the evening at Mrs. Curtiss James' was a most fashionable affair—and what is more a real success. I gave a talk and readings from *Victory*. One hour and a quarter with an ovation at the end. They were most attentive. Laughs at proper places and snuffles at the last when I read the whole chapter of Lena's death. It was a great social function and people fought for invitations.[1] I made it clearly understood from the first that I was not doing this sort of thing for money. This gave my visit to U. S. a particular character about which the press spoke out. Generally my reception in the papers was wonderful. F.N.D. himself is impressed.

My love to you,
J. CONRAD.

P.S. Leaving on motor tour New Eng^d and Boston on the 15th. About 10 days. Remember me to the Wedgwoods.

(1) Refers to the celebrated evening when Conrad made his one real public appearance in America.

The Copley-Plaza,
Boston,
Mass.
18. 5. 23.

Dearest Dick,

Just a line to tell you that I continue to be entertained in a princely fashion by the D's.[1] The articles on J. C. continue to appear, all friendly and in some sort respectful. D'y offers to guarantee £4,000 p.y. for 3 years—(and as much more as possible)—apart from serial-proceeds. I will tell you all the details when we meet.

The D's are coming over to see me home. We leave on the second June and ought to reach South'on on the 9th. ("Majestic.")

I hope, my dear fellow, you are keeping well and have no worries on your mind. In the midst of New England my thoughts are fixed on *England* (tout court), where my affections for my family and my friends dwell immovably.

We must meet very soon after my return. I would like [you] to come while I entertain the Doubledays. But of all that more anon.

My love to you,

Yrs,

J. CONRAD.

(1) The Doubledays.

Oswalds,
Bishopsbourne,
Kent.
June 25th. 1923.

My dear Dick,

Thank you very much for all the trouble and thought you give to the success of the Hour-glass Edition.[1] To tell you the truth, the Richmond idea[2] of giving a history of the books does not strike me as brilliant, as from its very nature it must be a second-hand thing. and, moreover, as those books are not depending upon any ideas, their genesis can not be made to appear important. Prefaces are in the light of personal confessions which can only interest somebody acquainted with the books, and it was on that assumption that they were written.

If you could say what sort of fiction mine is from the point of view of story-telling and hint at some characteristics, that, perhaps, would arouse curiosity. I am telling you what is in my mind, but I can have no possible objection to anything you wish to do. I am very sure that even on the historical side you will do something excellent and infinitely helpful.

By all means, my dear, do try to infuse some

---

(1) This title was dropped, and the edition, published by Doubleday, Page, is known as the Concord Edition.

(2) Refers to an article on the Uniform Edition, published by Dent. which I had undertaken to write for Bruce Richmond, editor of the *Times Literary Supplement.*

spirit of enterprise into . . . All your suggestion have my authority behind them. You may say that.

I don't know how to thank you for your unwearied friendship. Whatever you do will be well done.

Ever yours,

J. C.

Oswalds,
Bishopsbourne,
Kent.
July, 14th. 1923.

My dearest Dick,

I am returning you the article[1] with two corrections as to matters of fact and one of style.

As it stands I can have nothing against it.
As to my feelings that is a different matter; and I think
that, looking at the intimate character of our friendship and trusting to the indulgence of your affection, I
may disclose them to you without reserve.

My point of view is that this is an opportunity, if not unique then not likely to occur again in my
lifetime. I was in hopes that on a general survey it could
also be made an opportunity for me to get freed from
that infernal tail of ships, and that obsession of my sea
life which has about as much bearing on my literary existence, on my quality as a writer, as the enumeration of
drawing-rooms which Thackeray frequented could have
had on his gift as a great novelist. After all, I may have
been a seaman, but I am a writer of prose. Indeed, the
nature of my writing runs the risk of being obscured by
the nature of my material. I admit it is natural; but only
the appreciation of a special personal intelligence can
counteract the superficial appreciation of the inferior intelligence of the mass of readers and critics. Even Doubleday was considerably disturbed by that characteristic as
evidenced in press notices in America, where such headings as "Spinner of sea-yarns—master-mariner—seaman
writer" and so forth predominated. I must admit that

(1) This refers to the article mentioned in the previous letter.

the letter-press had less emphasis than the headings; but that was simply because they didn't know the facts. That the connection of my ships with my writings stands, with my concurrence I admit, recorded in your book is, of course, a fact. But that was biographical matter, not literary. And where it stands it can do no harm. Undue prominence has been given to it since, and yet you know yourself very well that in the body of my work barely one-tenth is what may be called sea stuff, and even of that, the bulk, that is *Nigger* and *Mirror*, has a very special purpose, which I emphasise myself in my Prefaces.

Of course, there are seamen in a good many of my books. That doesn't make them sea stories, any more than the existence of de Barral in *Chance* (and he occupies there as much space as Captain Anthony) makes that novel a story about the financial world. I do wish that all those ships of mine were given a rest, but I am afraid that when the Americans get hold of them they will never, never, never get a rest.

The summarising of Prefaces, though you do it extremely well, has got this disadvantage that it doesn't give their atmosphere, and indeed it can not give their atmosphere, simply because those pages are an intensely personal expression, much more so than all the rest of my writing, with the exception of the *Personal Record* perhaps. A question of policy arises there: whether it is a good thing to give people the bones, as it were. It may destroy their curiosity for the dish. I am aware, my dear Richard, that while talking over with you the forthcoming article, I used the word historical in connection with my fiction, or with my method, or something of the sort.

I expressed myself badly, for I certainly had not in my mind the history of the books. What I was thinking at the time was a phrase in a long article in the *Seccolo*. The critic remarked that there was no difference in method or character between my fiction and my professedly auto-biographical matter, as evidenced in the *Personal Record*. He concluded that my fiction was not historical, of course, but had an authentic quality of development and style, which in its ultimate effect resembled historical perspective.

My own impression is that what he really meant was that my manner of telling, perfectly devoid of familiarity as between author and reader, aimed essentially at the intimacy of a personal communication, without any thought for other effects. As a matter of fact, the thought for effects is there all the same (often at the cost of mere directness of narrative) and can be detected in my unconventional grouping and perspective, which are purely temperamental and wherein almost all my "art" consists. That, I suspect, has been the difficulty the critics felt in classifying it as romantic or realistic. Whereas, as a matter of fact, it is fluid, depending on grouping (sequence) which shifts, and on the changing lights giving varied effects of perspective.

It is in those matters gradually, but never completely, mastered that the history of my books really consists. Of course the plastic matter of this grouping and of those lights has its importance, since without it the actuality of that grouping and that lighting could not be made evident any more than Marconi's electric waves could be made evident without the sending-out and receiving instruments. In other words, without mankind, my art, an infinitesimal thing, could not exist.

All this, my dear fellow, has apparently no reference to your article, but truly enough is extracted from me by a consideration of your article. My dearest fellow, I can not (I would never dream!) tell you what to publish and what not to publish; but as far as America is concerned I am a little bit alarmed, for the reason stated above. I would take the privilege of our friendship to point out to you too that things written for a friend in a copy of a book, in a particular mood and in the assurance of not being misunderstood, look somewhat different in cold print.[2] And then I wonder whether, quoting me as an authority on myself, is a discreet thing to do. I always come back to my first statement, that this is an opportunity that will never be renewed in my life-time for the judgment of a man who certainly knows my work best and not less certainly is known for my closest intimate, but before all is the best friend my work has ever had.

Jessie and I are very delighted at your having met B. in that friendly manner, and by our good impression as to his health and his optimistic mood. My wrist has got achey again or else I would have written in pen and ink, and, I trust, expressed myself better,

Our love to you, Ever yours,

J. CONRAD.

---

(2) The reference is to the notes Conrad wrote for me in copies of his books, from which I was quoting in my article.

This whole letter is an admirable summary of Conrad's critical philosophy.

Oswalds,
July 17th 1923.

Dear Dick,

Thank you very much for your letter. I am afraid that my mind, being very full of your article[1] at this, what I consider a critical, period in the fate of my works, I absolutely forgot to thank you for the successful negotiation with the *Daily Mail;* though I meant to do it and, as a matter of fact, have been under the impression that I had done it. Eric had a letter from Macloud (?) and the thing is settled.[2] Thank you ever so much. The money, I think, from both sides won't be available till the end of the year, which is all right; for Eric will advance me the amount for doctor's bills (nearly £80 for the last quarter) and also in Sept. for the current quarter, which probably will not be quite so much. This is a bad time for me because I have to pay local taxes for the half year (some £35 and dressmaker's bill for about the same amount.

I am afraid, my dear, that you think that I am unduly worrying about the affair of publicity for my uniform edition here; but you understand that the moment is perhaps critical. It may fix my position with the buying public. I have always tried to counteract the danger of precise classification, either in the realm of exotism or of

(1) This is the article referred to in the two previous letters.

(2) This refers to an article "Christmas Day at Sea," which I had arranged with the *Daily Mail* to publish on Dec. 24th, 1923, and which is now included in *Last Essays.* The literary editor of the paper was then L. R. MacLeod.

the sea; and in the course of years here and there I have
had helpful paragraphs and articles in that sense. But
they never amounted to much. Neither were my protests
very effective. Truly I made no special efforts. But the
situation is now worth the trouble of special handling. I
don't mean on the point of literary appreciation, but
simply of *classification.* You know how the public mind
fastens on externals, on mere facts, such, for instance, as
ships and voyages, without paying attention to any deeper
significance they may have. If Richmond really wants this
you ought certainly to send it to him. But I should have
thought that his public is rather select and, in a sense,
literary. It certainly will draw attention to the Edition,
but the question is, in which way? I have visited many
foreign places and have been on board many ships. But so
has the author of "Captain Kettle," of whom it used to be
frequently stated that he "made a point of covering ten
thousand miles of new ground every year." The bulk of my
last letter to you, my dear Dick, was not so much a suggestion as a sort of thinking aloud, for which I feel called
to apologise, mainly on the ground that you knew all that
before, and indeed had thought all that out for yourself.
But if I may make a suggestion, what do you think of
this?—Suppose you opened by a couple of short paragraphs of general observation on authors and their
material, how they transform it from particular to general, and appeal to universal emotions by the temperamental handling of personal experience? You might also
say that not everybody can do that, and then you might
say "look at Conrad. whose new edition is coming out.

It is a case in point. His prefaces are now for the first time made accessible to the public, very characteristic of him and of special interest as he gives in many of them the genesis of the books, the history of initial suggestions. But all his stories expand far beyond their frame and appeal to no special public—looking for exotism, or adventure, or the sea—but to all of us who, etc. etc." . . . All this, of course, short, and even crude if you like. You do know how to write pregnant sentences. Then the rest of the article a little shortened, say, for instance, by cutting out all mention of stories of which I say distinctly I have no comment to make. Thus Richmond will get what he wants and you may save my hide from being permanently tarred.

This damned sea business keeps off as many people as it gathers in.[3] It may have been otherwise twenty-five years ago. Now the glamour is worn off and even twenty-five years ago the sea glamour did not do much for the *Nigger*.

But I daresay I am making all this fuss for nothing, and besides, no man can escape his fate.

A. Page[4] is coming here to-morrow, lunch, in a party of four.

Jessie sends her love.

Ever yours,
J. CONRAD.

(3) Most of this letter deals with my article for the *Times Literary Supplement*. Conrad had the greatest dislike of being taken for a mere writer of sea stories. Indeed, nothing irritated him more.

(4) Arthur Page, son of the former American Ambassador to Great Britain and one of the partners of Doubleday, Page.

[Oswalds.]
Monday. 22. 7. 23.

Dearest Dick,

The article as amended and added-to by you is first rate.[1]

I have ventured to compose the pars. relating to *M. of the S.* and *P.R.* If your conviction will let them stand I would be glad. In a few other places I ventured a line or two in pen and ink.

As to *No.* If I ever mentioned 12 hours it must relate to P. Cabello where I was ashore about that time. In La Guayra as I went up the hill and had a distant view of Caracas I must have been 2½ to 3 days. It's such a long time ago! And there were a few hours in a few other places on that dreary coast of Ven[la].[2]

Thanks a thousand times, my dear fellow, for your work and thought and your inexhaustible patience. We are looking forward to your arrival on Sat.—or will it be Friday? Please drop me a line.

Would you mind to have the article typed in 2 cop. at my expense?

Ever affec[ly] yours,
J. CONRAD.

---

(1) See the three previous letters.

(2) This is a very interesting paragraph, as showing the short space of time in which he gathered atmosphere for *Nostromo* on the Venezuelan coast.

Oswalds,
Bishopsbourne,
Kent.
30. 7. 23.

Dearest Dick,

Ever so many thanks for your letter and enclosure.

It had been nice to have you here if only for a few hours.

Mr. and Mrs. A. B. Conrad turned up suddenly in the afternoon—in quite good spirits, but still homeless.

A. B. most appreciative of your friendliness. As he can get away for five days, they are coming here on Friday to stay with us (instead of B'stairs) on their own, as it were, with perfect liberty of movement. They seem to like the idea—which was Jessie's.

She sends you her love.

Ever yours,
J. CONRAD.

Don't forget to present my duty.

Oswalds,
Bishopsbourne,
Kent.
28. 8. 23. 6.30 p.m.

My dear Dick,

I had a letter from the editor of *B.P.*[1] He will want the MS. by the 15th next, and that will be all right. I will have the thing done by to-morrow, I suppose. His letter has been acknowledged and the little photograph of the hole in the bow of the "Torrens" enclosed.

He didn't mention in his letter anything about reproducing the MS. or about a photograph of myself, but I certainly have no objection. He must, however, get the photograph from Annan[2] himself, as the man took those negatives for nothing and ought to have his fee. There are several of them, but the one from No. 1 negative is the best.

Will you, my dear fellow, tell Hook[3] that on the telephone, as my answer has gone.

Thank you very much for putting this affair through with such speed and efficiency. And, of course, the revelation of his readiness to jump at an occasional contribution from me is extremely valuable.[4] I hope you have

---

(1) The *Blue Peter,* for which Conrad was writing an article on the "Torrens," now included in *Last Essays.*

(2) The photograph taken by Annan in Glasgow on the day on which Conrad sailed for America.

(3) F. A. Hook, owner and editor of the *Blue Peter.*

(4) He was a friend of mine and was, of course, only too pleased to get an article from Conrad.

got into the shafts of the Carmelite cart and that the harness doesn't gall.

Jessie sends her love.

Yours ever,

J. CONRAD.

Dearest Dick,

You must be surprised not to have heard from me before about the *Times* article. As a matter of fact I was working at the *B.P.* article and would not look at the *Supplement* till I had finished—which was done last night.

Many thanks, my dear fellow. Your historic survey of Mr. C's books looks and reads magnificently. Your view as to what it should have been is gorgeously vindicated by the execution. I can't imagine anything that could have been better for its purpose. And I must say that Richmond has been most generous with his space. The display is distinctly impressive, and the "head" and "tail" pieces of writing are done in your best manner both as to sobriety and eloquence of expression. I can not thank you sufficiently.[1]

I have written to-day to Hook to tell him that he will have the article on the 10th. It is absolutely ready now, but he must not be led to think that I do those things too easily. It took just three days from the first inception to the completing a copy fit for the printer. Easy money, you may think. But the trouble is that it is all, as it were, expended before I even get hold of it. A damnable coil to be tangled in.

I have besides a lot of small bills, the January journey to Havre before me. As Mrs. C. insists on going

---

(1) My article in the *Times Literary Supplement* appeared on Aug. 30th, 1923. See letters of June 25th, July 14th, July 17th, and July 22nd, 1923.

over too, the programme will be: arriving in London on the 10th, leaving for Havre by the night service on the 11th, returning from Havre by the night service on the 15th—in which case I will have the company of Aubry, who returns to London for a month or two on that date. To tell you the truth I dread the enterprise, for I get very nervous and tired when I have to look after anybody. We take John with us, of course, but we won't leave him in France, because the Rev. Bost and his family don't return to their house in Havre till the end of Sept.[2] They will come up for the day on the 12th, from their country house to see us in Havre.

Eric is back and I have arranged to see him on Monday to talk over various business matters (damn them), while we lunch together, probably at one. But I will be at the R.A.C. before 12, and if this reaches you in time I hope you will step in and cheer me up by some optimistic talk. I will have with me a clean copy of: "The Torrens: A Personal Tribute," By Joseph Conrad—[3] so that you may read it at your leisure. And I would like to consult you in that connection on a matter I need not state here.

Jessie sends her love.

Ever yours,

J. CONRAD.

---

(2) John Conrad stayed for some time at Havre for the purpose of learning French in the house of a French Protestant clergyman.

(3) This article appeared in the *Blue Peter* of October, 1923.

160

[Oswalds.]
7. 9. 23.

My dear Dick,

I have your letter. Many thanks.

We'll arrive at the Curzon for lunch and hope you will share the "modest repast" (vin ordinaire).

I have given up the idea of writing to the *Suppl*ᵗ about Sir F's communication, since you are willing to say something.[1] I have no locus standi in this affair, really.

Ever yours,

J. CONRAD.

We are coming up on Sunday only because Mama Piper[2] has collapsed with a bad throat. I will be awfully bored unless you bring me an interesting book or two (on loan, I mean).

---

(1) Sir Frank Swettenham published in the *Times Literary Supplement* of 6th September a letter about the character of Lord Jim referred to in my article. Conrad in conversation with me took strong exception to his attitude, and I published a letter, in which I expressed disagreement with Sir Frank, in the Supplement of 13th September. Sir Frank replied in the issue of 20th September, and Messrs. Alfred Holt, the steamship owners of Liverpool, gave the true history of the pilgrim ship in. a letter in the issue of 11th October.

(2) The Conrads' cook.

Oswalds,
Bishopsbourne,
Kent.
20. 9. 23.

My dearest Dick,

Jessie and I are grieved and ashamed. But most of all we are thunderstruck. Why! of course we did *not* see you in town when on our way home. But by a strange aberration of thought we were under the impression that we had! It's too absurd for words, and I hope you will keep it quiet or else the world will say that both Jessie and I are in an advanced stage of senile decay.[1] The delusion was so complete that when I saw the 1st. domes^c servant article[2] I wondered why you did not tell me that they were coming. Quite good stuff.

We passed through town on Sunday, arriving home at 4.30 p.m.; and at 5.30 I was in bed with a temperature and that dreadful asthma cough which reduces me to despair. It was beginning before we went over. I am down-stairs now and was going to drop you a line to-day, but I don't feel well.

Our love and regrets.

Ever yours,
J. C.

P.S. *Let us know the earliest day you can run over.* I am going early to bed to-day.

---

(1) This is typical of Conrad's concern at an accidental piece of neglect.

(2) Refers to a series of articles I was writing for the *Daily Mail*.

Jessie stood the trip well. Enjoyed it. Arrangements are made. Serious, spartan French family. I am quite pleased, but Mr. John[8] is pulling a long face rather.

(8) See letter of September 1 and note (4).

[Oswalds.]
Wedy, [Sept. 28?]

Dearest Dick,

The water being cut off for 3 days at the main on account of the pipe-connections which must be renewed, we are migrating to the Curzon[1] to-morrow.

Jessie is coming by road. I'll be at the R.A.C. about 12 for ½ an hour on my way to Pinker with whom I'll lunch. I hope I'll see you or have a message from you there.

Our love.

Yours,
J. C.

(1) In his later years Conrad usually stayed at the Curzon Hotel when in London.

Dearest Dick,

I have been in an awful quandary about the frontispiece for the *Nigger of the N.* in the Concord edition.

The latest brain-wave is to get a photo on Tower Hill which would include part at least of the front of the Mint—where the crew part from each other.

It seems impossible to find such a thing in photo shops. We are trying still. But in case we fail do you think you could get the *D*^{y} *Mail* photographer to take for me such a picture with a view to reproduction in U.S.?[1] I am prepared, of course, to pay a fee.

I am bothering [you] simply because I feel that it ought to be done by a skilled person. I hope you won't mind. They are in a hurry over there and I should like to catch next *Wednesday's* packet. Our love.

Ever yours,

J. CONRAD.

---

(1) I got the photograph taken for him and it now serves as a frontispiece to *The Nigger of the "Narcissus"* in the Concord Edition.

Oswalds,
Bishopsbourne,
Kent.
5. 10. 23.

Dearest Dick,

Many thanks for your unwearied kindness in this, as in other, matters. I suppose I can't hope to have the print in time for the next Wed^y packet?

Should it reach your hands on Tuesday, pray, my dear fellow, post it straight to Garden City. Just write on back: *Nigger front^{ce} from J. C.*[1] . . . is great. Really you are very good in that column.[2]

Our love.

Yours,
J. C.

P.S. So sorry your last Vailimas have been delayed. They came yesterday. Going to-night.

---

(1) See previous letter and note.
(2) Articles I was writing under a pseudonym for the *Daily Mail*.

[Oswalds.]
Wedy. [Oct. 1923.]

Dearest Dick,

Herewith 30/—for the camera man.[1]

Jessie says she wrote to you yesterday. Do drop us a line.

I got up last Sat. after 4 days in bed and have [been] at work since Monday.[2] Very slow though.

We heard from John, who arrived safely.

Ever yours,

J. C.

---

(1) The man who took the photograph which forms the frontispiece to *The Nigger of the "Narcissus"* in the Concord Edition. See two previous letters.

(2) On *Suspense* presumably.

[Oswalds.]
25 Oct. 23.

Dearest Dick,

Thanks for your note. I'll await H's¹ communication before thinking of the subject, in the hope of
receiving a helpful hint from him.

We were delighted by the good news. Yes my
dear, you made a very good thing of the Simple Life.²

Ever yrs,

J. CONRAD.

Jessie's love.

---

(1) J. A. Hammerton of the Amalgamated Press, London, who
wanted Conrad to write an article for him. See note (1) to next
letter.

(2) Refers to an ironical article I had written.

Oswalds,
Bishopsbourne,
Kent.
Nov. 2nd. 1923.

Dearest Dick,

In the words of the parrot after the monkey pulled all the feathers out of its tail, I have had "a hell of a time." I am dictating this from bed. The pain is less to-day, but I am not fit for much and I am very anxious about things.

I had a letter from Hammerton, which I have answered at once. From what he says the time is rather short and I haven't more than 1,200 words of the article written. I shall try to work a little to-day. What it will be like, God only knows. I am rather glad in answering H. I suggested that 4,000 words might be enough for that introduction and that he could proportionately reduce the fee.[1]

Herewith the 20 signed copies.[2] I have kept No. 3 for myself, as I like to have it here. I did not inscribe No. 1 specially to you; I just signed it like the

(1) J. A. Hammerton had planned a serial publication in many parts to be called *Countries of the World*. He asked me to write some articles for it, and I suggested that he should try to get Conrad to write a general preface. He jumped at the idea, and Conrad consented to do it. It appeared, under the title of "The Romance of Travel," in the first number, February, 1924. In *Last Essays* it is printed under the title of "Geography and Some Explorers."

(2) This refers to the privately printed pamphlet which I had had made of his "Torrens" article.

others, but if you want me to make some additions, it can be done later. I know that you will see to it that Wise gets his copy, and Hook also. Perhaps you would like to give No. 5 to somebody you know. Of the remaining 15 the proceeds of ten would be for me. It is only fair that you should participate in things which are put in my way by you, especially this windfall, for which certainly I have not done a stroke of work.

        Jessie sends her love.

                Yours ever,

                    J. CONRAD.

P.S. *S. Agent* will be performed at the Leeds Art Theatre next Monday week, under the direction of Laurie Ramsden, to whom I gave permission a few months ago. I hear that there is much curiosity awakened there. I only wish I had somebody who could give me a trustworthy report of the performance. There will be, I believe, six of them.

Dearest Dick,

Many thanks. You really can't (and *ought
not*) object to the enclosed. Had I been able to move I
would have gone miles to find some object I could have
presented to you in memory of the "Torrens" transaction,
which was a pleasant affair altogether. It would have
been prettier, no doubt, but when I reflect that if I had
made an early marriage I could have been (easily) father
of a man of your age, this way seems permissible between
you and me.

I am getting into a funk about Hammerton.
I'll see how much I will do by to-morrow even^g, for I am
going to start work to-day. If I don't get on and do not
feel fit, it would be only decent to tell him.[1]

Jessie sends her love.

Ever yours,

J. C.

---

(1) He did succeed in writing the article: see previous letter and
note (1).

[Oswalds.]
Monday. [Nov., 1923.]

Dearest Dick,

Thanks for the send-off in the *D. M.* to-day.[1]
I do want you to come this week-end, but I don't think I
am equal to "company." I am by no means well yet. So
perhaps we will put off Sartoris'[2] visit to better times. It
could be no pleasure to see a man groaning in a dressing
gown.

I wonder what the fate of the *R.*[3] will be?
Your copy Ed. de Luxe is waiting for you here.

Ever yours,

J. C.

---

(1) The reference is to the review of *The Rover* which I wrote
for the *Daily Mail*.

(2) My friend, G. L. Sartoris, accompanied me down to Conrad's
for a week-end at a later date.

(3) *The Rover.*

Oswalds,
Nov. 12th. 1923.

Dearest Dick,

I am sure you will be fraternally pleased to
hear that I have this moment—4.20 p.m.—finished my
"Geographical" introduction,[1] the light of day dying out
of the window as line succeeded line on the last page.

You know I always turn to you to make life
easy for me in certain ways, so perhaps you won't be
surprised if I ask you to give Hammerton to understand
that I should like to be paid on the delivery of the MS.,
I mean, of course, within the week or something of that
kind. I have done it in full as agreed, 5,000 words and
perhaps 100 over, and I assure you I earned the money
by the effort I had to put into it, both before I was laid
up and during that time, and afterwards too. For my
convalescence was by no means good and to-day is the
first day on which I do not feel absolutely ill, though I
have been actually at work ever since last Thursday.

I had Fox[2] to come and see me, and the fact
of the matter is that the action of the heart is not satisfactory. "Flabby heart," he calls it in his horrid way. As
a matter of fact the organ is tired, and must have been
growing so for the last 18 months perhaps, with the strain
and worry of one thing after another—but you know
the history of the last 18 months as well as I do—and
now it betrays its condition by fluttering and missing

(1) This refers to the article for Hammerton mentioned pre-
viously.

(2) Dr. Fox of Ashford, who had long attended him.

about every fourth beat. This accounts for that unshake-
able despondency of which I complained to you more than
once; for there is nothing organically wrong to account
for it. However, I repeat that I am better to-day, and the
only thing I dread is the persistence of the cough, which
has played a considerable part in bringing me low.

I can do no more to-day and I will take a full
two days to revise the article, of which Miss H.[3] will make
a clean copy. We expect to send it off to Hammerton on
Thursday. You may communicate to him the good news,
for I imagine he may be wondering at the delay.

And now it's done let me thank you, my dear
fellow, for shoving the thing in my way. It's obvious that
for some time I have not been fit to grapple with the
novel,[4] and it was a great moral comfort to have some
work to do which I was capable of doing; not to speak of
the material convenience of having the extra money which
was very much needed and would have had to be obtained
outside the provision of the normal budget. A necessity
which worried me exceedingly.

I trust you were not annoyed with us for
putting off your visit here with Sartoris. You see what
was behind it. A really rather low physical state, with
unpleasant sensations, coupled with a desperate resolve
to get the Hammerton thing through. S. would have had
a dismal time and I simply did not feel equal to seeing a
comparative stranger, who, as a matter of fact, I like
very much. We should be glad if you found an early

---

(3) Miss Hallowes, his secretary.

(4) *Suspense.*

opportunity of bringing him down here, and in any case we hope to see you here before Dec. 15th. Jessie may have to run up to London to see Sir Robert.[5] She looks well but I am rather worried about the constant exasperating twitching of the great muscle, which is the sort of thing that may bring on a nervous breakdown. She sends you her love.

Yours ever,

J. CONRAD.

---

(5) Sir Robert Jones, the surgeon.

Oswalds,
Bishopsbourne,
Kent.
[Nov., 1923.]

Dearest Dick,

Thanks for yours. Of course Jessie and I will be delighted if you can come with Sartoris as you suggest.

The after-effects of my last fit of gout were more pronounced than usual. I had Fox over to see me. Nothing fundamentally serious. I am much better.

We dispatched the article of full length (5,500 w. about) yesterday to Hammerton. I hope he will find it suitable. It was rather a grind—yet in a sense I was glad I had something to do when obviously not fit to work at the novel.

The *Times* has given all the principal figures reached at that idiotic sale.[1] What it has done for me is that I have suddenly become known to lots of people who had never heard of me before. Yes, I agree with you that the price of future MS. will be affected favourably. But there are no MS! I haven't heard from Wise. I don't think he expected such an enormous boost.

All the luck to you in the campaign.

Ever yours,
J. C.

Jessie sends her love.

---

(1) The Quinn sale in New York, where Conrad MSS. fetched enormously high prices.

[Oswalds.]

17. 12. 23.

Dearest Dick,

I haven't yet shaken off the trouble—but the improvement, if slow, will be lasting.

Fox has been over and we have arranged a treatment to be followed for 4 or 6 weeks directly all the acute symptoms are gone. Of course I feel as tho' I had been ill. But, as a matter of fact, the heart-action is quite normal now, the lungs are clear, pulse and temp. have been normal for some time already and my blood-pressure is quite satisfactory. In fact, my arteries are younger than my age.

When can we expect you here? I have been wondering as to your health. Please let us know. Have you seen Gwatkin?[1] His novel is not bad and I can see now why it had that sale.[2] Shall I send it to you—or has he given you a copy?

Up to Dec. F.U.[3] disposed of 26,000 cop. of *The R.* 18,000 in U.K. and 8,000 Colonial—in round numbers (1st. imp.). I have heard that the booksellers in this part of the country can no longer procure 1st impression copies.

Love,

J. C.

---

(1) F. Ashton-Gwatkin, whose father was the Vicar of Bishopsbourne.

(2) *Kimono.*

(3) Fisher Unwin, the publisher of *The Rover.*

Oswalds,
Bishopsbourne,
Kent.
27. Dec. 23.

Dearest Dick,

I am awaiting with impatience the announcement of your visit. Things are not so well here. Jessie is menaced with an abscess in the upper part of the leg— (deep in), but the doctor is not certain. If it isn't that, then it must be something equally serious. Reid[1] assured me there was no immediate cause for anxiety. He is coming to see her to-morrow and then will notify Sir R. Jones.

J. is, as usual, cheerfully facing it upstairs with fomentations on her leg. But I am sure that inwardly she is feeling a bitter disappointment at what she calls "another set-back."

Don't allude to the state of my mind when you answer this—as Mrs. C. expects to be shown your letters.

Ever yours,

J. Conrad.

There is a bottle of Tobermory whisky awaiting you here. Jessie would not send it for fear of breakage.[2]

---

(1) Dr. Whitehead Reid of Canterbury.

(2) I always got a Christmas present from the Conrads.

Dear Dick,

     You shall have your Concord Set from me. The first 2 vols. *(Jim—Vic.)* have arrived this morning and I'll initial them for you. (thus$^{R. C.}_{J. C.}$)[1]

Ever yrs,

J. CONRAD.

---

(1) Conrad kept his word. The first volume is signed in full with his name and my name, and in all the other volumes, up to the time of his death—upwards of twenty—are our two sets of initials in his handwriting.

Oswalds.
Jan. 14th. 1924.

Dearest Dick,

I hasten to tell you that I am very grateful for every tactful step you have taken in this matter. I must confess I had some slight qualms about Wise.[1] Your action has done away with them, and of course you cannot doubt I am animated by the most friendly sentiments towards T.J.W. Of course I will sign and annotate his copy with pleasure.[2]

I can now tell you definitely that we are coming up on Wednesday, hour uncertain. I could certainly take you out to the R.A.C., but then, my dear, I am not quite right yet, and I don't know whether I will be fit at the end of the journey. This is the hard truth. Naturally we expect you to drop in at any time and on any occasion when you feel like it.

Thanks once more.

Love from us both.

Yrs,

J. C.

P.S. Sir R. J.'s[3] visit fixed for 11 o'clock Thursday.

---

(1) This concerns, I think, the sale of the MS. of his article *Georgaphy and Some Explorers.* He probably thought that Wise had already as many Conrad MSS. as he wanted.

(2) His copy of *The Rover.*

(3) Sir Robert Jones.

Hotel Curzon,
Curzon Street,
Mayfair,
London. W.
Wedy. 10.30. [January, 1924.]

Dearest Dick,

Sir Robert appointed to-morrow, Thursday, 10.30 for his visit to Jessie.

We have been to see B's home and child. The baby is really quite nice.[1] Everything looks quite satisfactory there. Saw B for a moment about one o'clock. He is happy no doubt and looks less strained than ever I've seen him look for the last 4 years.

I hope you'll 'phone me a message early in the morning. After Sir R. J. has been my time is yours. Will you lunch?

Ever yours,
J. C.

---

(1) Conrad took a real pleasure in his grandchild. He insisted on the baby being brought to him when he was dying.

[Oswalds.]
1st Feb^y '24.

My dear Dick,

My report is that I am better, but poor Jessie has not improved much. She was pleased with your S's letters.[1] We enjoyed your week-end with us very much.

Perhaps Jessie has told you that your sister and Col. Ruston called on us on Sunday. We were very pleased to see them. R. apparently is about to sail to Austr^a on business.

I have tackled the novel to-day.[2] What a lot of work there is to do yet! However, I feel not so very much disgusted. 30 pp. *will have to* come out. But that's my least trouble. I feel fairly hopeful.

Ever yours,
J. C.

---

(1) My sister's letters to her.

(2) The reference is to *Suspense,* on which Conrad was then working with great difficulty.

[Oswalds.]
4 Mch. '24.

Dearest Dick,

I had a letter from Sir Hugh Clifford. He sends me six copies of his address to the Legislative Council.[1] One of them I retain and the other five I am sending to you as requested by H.C. *with his love.* He asks you to give one to your brother, one to Col. Ingles,[2] and the other two to any one you may know who is interested in African affairs—as a counterblast to the nasty fairy tales which my Lord of the Western Isles[3] has been uttering lately about the Colony. H.C. will arrive about end March. The report is very interesting. He gives me Ap. 25 or May 2 as dates for a week-end visit. I suppose you will join us. No hurry to fix it yet.

Ever yours,

J. CONRAD.

P.S. If you have already a copy perhaps Wise would like this.

(1) Sir Hugh Clifford was then Governor of Nigeria.

(2) My brother, J. H. Curle, and Colonel Ingles had travelled out to Nigeria in the same ship with Sir Hugh Clifford.

(3) Lord Leverhulme, who had recently visited Nigeria.

Oswalds,
Bishopsbourne,
Kent.
10th March, 1924.

Many happy returns, my dearest Dick.[1] We
expect to see you next week-end. Meantime we shall drink
your health to-morrow in "good red wine."
Yours with great affection,

J. CONRAD.

---

(1) My birthday is on March 11th.

Dearest Dick,

The Hudson Ed. went off last Sat. in four parcels. How good of you to let me unload this affair on your overcharged shoulders.

To-day's . . . was indeed good—for the subject was not easy to treat being within the borders of psychology. The bust of Ep. has grown truly monumental. It is a marvellously effective piece of sculpture, with even something more than masterly interpretation in it. The cast will be made probably on Friday.[1]

The Keating Collection will be held here for your inspection. You'll find the items in the study, but each wrapped up on account of the dust. Come when you like (with notice) but in any case I don't intend to return it for a month—even if completed by signatures, etc. before that time.[2]

Jessie sends her love.

Yours ever,
J. C.

---

(1) This reference is to the bust Jacob Epstein was then making of Conrad.

(2) Conrad had consented to write notes in the collection of his works formed by George T. Keating, the American collector.

[Oswalds.]
Thursday. [May 1, 1924.]

Dearest Dick,

Delighted to hear you are coming for lunch on Sat.

I am very glad you have asked E.P.[1] and his wife to lunch next Thursday. It's very kind of you.

Jessie sends her love. She has been upstairs for 3 days so as to rest her leg, which is giving her a lot of pain when she moves. I am improving slowly. What news there are I am keeping for your ear when you come.

Ever yours,
J. C.

---

(1) Eric Pinker. It was to dinner I had asked his wife and himself.

[Oswalds.]
Dearest Dick, [May, 1924.]

Here everything is much the same. No date yet. It is very good and dear of you to promise to stand by me in the coming trial[1] (and it will be that for me) in this more than brotherly fashion. I am very touched and very grateful.

On the actual day B. promised to come down early. John will be wired for in time too to see her just before the operation. It is Jessie's own wish. She is much comforted by the thought of your unfailing friendship towards us all. I am looking forward to a visit from you while she is in the Nurs. Home.[2] I can't shake off a sort of vague dread, tho' I agree with you that there is nothing else for it. The situation as it is cannot last. Neither am I without hope of complete success.

Eric and his wife were delighted with your entertainment. E. thinks you make a delightful host, while the company was pleasant beyond his expectations. Was *our* Gov. Gen. in good form?[3] E. was much struck by his amiability.

Jessie sends her love.

Ever yrs,

J. CONRAD.

(1) Mrs. Conrad's imminent operation.

(2) I made this visit and stayed for three days with Conrad while his wife was in the nursing home at Canterbury. It was my last visit to him before the one during which he died, and was made particularly pleasant by a Sunday visit from his old friend, R. B. Cunninghame Graham.

(3) Sir Hugh Clifford.

P.S. I had a satisfactory letter from Nelson Doubleday. I have sent them a preface for the Vol. of Coll^d Stories.[4]

---

(4) A Selection of Conrad's short stories had been made for a one-volume edition to which he wrote a special introduction, now included in *Last Essays*.

[Oswalds.]
[10th June, 1924.]

Dearest Dick,

Jessie was *so* pleased with your encouraging letter!

I will be in London to-morrow (Wed.) but will make no call on your time as I remember you telling me Wed. was a heavy day with you.

The object of my visit will be only to lunch at the Polish Legation (at 1.30).[1] I will travel up by car, as I shirk the rail. I am certain to be [at] R.A.C. a little after 12 noon and if you can spare the time for a social drink it would be nice. Do you think you would be able to come down here next week-end? But perhaps that would be too dismal. I'll send you word directly the $op\text{-}er^{on}$ is over.

Ever yrs,
J. CONRAD.

---

(1) Conrad was pleased with this invitation to lunch at the Polish Legation and enjoyed the experience.

Oswalds,
Bishopsbourne,
Kent.
Wedy. 2 July. 6.30 p.m. [1924.]

Dearest Dick,

Any chance of your coming down here on, say, Friday ev^g for the week-end?

If you do, bring me a couple of books—not novels. I have had a severe cold and sub-acute bronchitis which left me like a rag. Am trying to fight off a fit of severe depression which has taken me by the throat, as it were. Hard luck.

Just came back from a visit to Mrs. C.[1] She is chirpy. Great luck.

Ever yours,
J. CONRAD.

---

(1) Mrs. Conrad was still in the nursing home in Canterbury, recovering from her operation.

[Oswalds.]
8. July. 1. p.m. [1924.]

Dearest Dick,

May I expect you on Friday ev^g? Please drop me a line so that I may warn Vinten[1] for "late duty."

Jessie goes on well, but her return home may be delayed beyond the first estimate for another week. I find life rather dismal now without John.

The article will be all right. It will have to do with Sailors, Saints, University Dons, etc., subjects of Legend.[2]

Ever yours,
(Signed) J. CONRAD.

---

(1) Conrad's chauffeur.
(2) This is the article called "Legends" which Conrad left unfinished. It was published in the *Daily Mail* a short time after his death, and has been reprinted in *Last Essays*.

22. 7. 24.

Dearest Curle,

   Thanks for your letter. Mrs. C. is coming home on Thursday which is cheering, tho' she will have to lay up for a week or two longer in her room upstairs.

   I am not getting on very well with my paper,[1] but it will be not very long now before it is finished. Do, dear Dick, send me that book of travels in Arabia I asked you for. I've nothing to read.

   Thanks for the return of the French book. I am slightly gouty in one hand and the corresponding foot.

      Ever affect^{ly} yours,

      J. C.

---

(1) "Legends." See previous letter and note (2).

The following telegram was the last communication I had from Conrad. I went down for the week-end on the night of Friday, August 1st, and found him apparently very well. On the morning of August 2nd he was seized with illness and on the morning of August 3rd he died from heart failure.

31 July, 1924.

Curle, 57 Russell Square, London.
Delighted, if you will put up with John's room.
Philip[1] and Co. will be here.

CONRAD.

---

(1) Conrad's grandson.